D0502652

In *Rock-Solid Volunteers*, Larry Fowler turns to one of Scripture's most successful leaders to unearth timeless solutions for recruiting, training, motivating and retaining volunteers. The life lessons my friend and colleague gleans from the first four chapters of Nehemiah are powerful, practical and applicable to any church ministry. By putting these principles and ideas into practice, your ministry team will soon brim with passionate, loyal volunteers who serve with excellence—and stick around.

JACK EGGAR, President/CEO, Awana®

I was highly encouraged, challenged and motivated to be a more effective leader by the parallels this book draws between the leadership style of Nehemiah and today's leadership challenges. This is a book that is full of practical tools that can help every leader in any size church or demographic background. I recommend that *Rock-Solid Volunteers* be a book on every leader's read list and in every church staff's library.

DENISE KISSEE, Director of Elementary Education
First Baptist Church, Woodstock, Georgia

Using the scriptural foundation of the leader Nehemiah, Larry provides fresh insight into calling people to ministry rather than simply recruiting to fill a position. I found the book full of fresh perspective and new ideas to help every children's ministry leader. It is obvious that Larry has personally experienced the difficulties of recruiting and caring for volunteers, and he shares from that wealth in a manner that everyone working with volunteers can draw from.

JOHN TIETSORT, TH.M., National Director, eChuchDepot
Chairman of the Board, International Network of Children's Ministry

I will be forever grateful for all of the volunteers at our local church that mentored and directed my son, Sam Towns, into fulltime Christian service. Without the sacrificial gift of "volunteers," Sam would not have gone on to finish his doctor's degree and become one of the great teachers here at Liberty University before he was killed in an automobile accident eight years ago. I fully recommend this book to everyone who works in Awana and everyone who works in a local church. Praise God for all volunteers who serve Christ in the Church.

ELMER L. TOWNS, Co-Founder and Vice President, Liberty University
Dean, Liberty Baptist Theological Seminary
Dean, School of Religion, Lynchburg, Virginia

ROCK
SOLID
VOLUNTEERS

HELLO
my name is

Larry Fowler

Executive Director of Program and Training, Awana®

Regal

From Gospel Light
Ventura, California, U.S.A.

Published by Regal
From Gospel Light
Ventura, California, U.S.A.
www.regalbooks.com
Printed in the U.S.A.

Library of Congress Cataloging-in-Publication Data
Fowler, Larry.
Rock-solid volunteers / Larry Fowler.
p. cm.
ISBN 978-0-8307-5745-9 (hardcover)
1. Lay ministry. 2. Church management. 3. Voluntarism—Management. I. Title.
BV677.F69 2010
253—dc22
2010044995

1 2 3 4 5 6 7 8 9 10 11 12 13 14 15 16 / 22 21 20 19 18 17 16 15 14 13 12 11 10

Rights for publishing this book outside the U.S.A. or in non-English languages are administered by Gospel Light Worldwide, an international not-for-profit ministry. For additional information, please visit www.glww.org, email info@glww.org, or write to Gospel Light Worldwide, 1957 Eastman Avenue, Ventura, CA 93003, U.S.A.

To order copies of this book and other Regal products in bulk quantities, please contact us at 1-800-446-7735.

CONTENTS

PREFACE

"I'm stepping down."

Can you think of three words dreaded much more by a ministry leader? You probably can, but I'm sure you agree with me—these are right near the top of nearly everyone's list. Just when you think you have a team in place, you get The Phone Call—the "I'm Stepping Down" Phone Call—and you end up frantically trying to fill a hole at the last minute. Absenteeism in general is a problem, but we really dread the constant challenge of replacing workers who leave their responsibilities, often with little or no advance notice.

Debbie, the children's ministry director at our church, heard those words this past Sunday. A couple of teachers just didn't show up. When she called to find out why, one of them said, "Oh, Debbie, I'm sorry I didn't tell you—*I'm stepping down*." Debbie was frustrated about having to find a last-minute substitute (which usually means that she or her husband steps in). She expressed her frustration this way: "You know what I'm doing, Larry? I'm supposed to *direct* the children's ministry. But that's not the way I feel. I'm simply the number one substitute! It seems nearly every week, someone is absent and doesn't tell me, or someone quits and I have to fill in. I love working with the kids, but *this is not what I'm supposed to be doing*." Debbie has to deal with her growing concern over whether or not the teachers are really committed. Her trust in their commitment is weakened. What does she do?

Pastors hear those words. Rick, a pastor friend who also teaches in a seminary, believes God has called him to lead churches from complacency back to vitality. He recently took on a new church located in an upper-middle-class neighborhood that he thought had great potential. It had nice facilities and seemed to be a fairly stable congregation (the previous pastor had retired after a couple of decades). When I asked Rick how ministry was going, his response was one I'll not soon forget. He took a long breath and let it out slowly. After about a five-second pause, he said, "Well, I'm just trying to keep the church out of the casket." He traced his discouragement

and frustration back to a familiar source. People, he said, were too
tired to work, and they were unwilling to start any new outreach.
He had never struggled before to motivate people, but *this* church
was really testing his calling. Not only were the people digging in
their heels if he suggested anything new, but they were also quitting
the ministries that were already going—just punching out and not
punching back in. Rick was worn out from hearing those dreaded
"I'm stepping down" words. "They'll support me verbally when I
suggest something, but follow through? I can't get anyone to take
any leadership." Could he have done anything differently?

My friend Jerry hears those words, too. Jerry oversees children's
ministry in a mega-church. Filling slots, covering for absent teachers, and recruiting new workers occupy a majority of his hours. He
is frustrated. He wants to do more profitable things in his position,
but his time is swallowed up with phone calls and emails about the
next week's ministry responsibilities. Jerry spends a great deal of
time just getting acquainted with new staff members, and he wor-
ries that he is sacrificing quality because the demand to fill slots is
so high. His senior pastor expects to have top-notch programs provided during each of three weekly worship services, and Jerry feels
like he's being stretched on a medieval rack. The turnover of leadership is about to kill him, he says. "I've got to find ways to keep
people committed to their ministry longer." What can he do?

I've heard those words many times. I work with Awana, a ministry that serves churches by providing programming, training and
materials for the purpose of evangelizing and discipling children
and youth. We have the pleasure of knowing that, around the
world, more than 400,000 volunteers serve in our ministry in more
than 20,000 churches. Keeping those workers engaged in ministry
is a primary, vital concern for us. At the time I am writing this
manuscript, we are enjoying unprecedented growth internation-
ally—volunteers committed to reaching children are stepping up at
a dizzying pace: There has been growth by tens of thousands each
year for the last few years. Even as we rejoice over so many new volunteers joining us, our concern is, can we keep them? Will they
continue in their ministry roles once the newness has worn off?

In the churches that use Awana as a ministry, recruitment is an annual event: Most churches enlist their volunteers for a school-year-long commitment. This means that every spring, as the school year finishes, our leadership around the world ends the club season, concerned about whether their people will serve another year. Then at the end of summer, recruitment often comes up short—sometimes positions are filled at the last minute, and sometimes they remain empty even as the school year begins. God continues to amaze us by providing this huge army of volunteers. Yet, while God provides, we still deal with understaffed ministries. Understaffed ministries nearly always struggle. Some die. We wonder, "What can we do?"

Recruiting people for ministry and keeping them engaged are perennial problems. So we ministry leaders often look for the newest thing—the most recent solution. We look at the biggest churches, or churches with the most charismatic leadership, and then try to copy what they do. This can be a very effective approach, assuming we make good choices about which individuals or programs we seek to emulate.

The Nebraska-Oklahoma football game of November 25, 1971, is known by some college football fans (especially if you're from Nebraska, as I am) as the Game of the Century. Since college football has pretty much only existed for a century, one could even call it the Game of All Time. I was just a teenager at the time, but this game, which pitted my #1-ranked Huskers against the #2-ranked Sooners, transformed me into a life-long fanatic. My team came out on top, 35-31, in a phenomenal seesaw game that propelled them to a second consecutive national championship. Since then, great teams and great games have been measured against that one. The Huskers had established a new standard of effectiveness, and for years afterward, other coaches came to Nebraska to study their techniques and learn to build their own programs more successfully.

Finding and keeping volunteers is a lot like sports, in the sense that "you win some; you lose some." Some teams of ministry leaders have great records, while others seem to lose more often than they win. When someone does a great job in ministry, why wouldn't others want to study what they do in order to get better? As with football, we have a natural desire to learn from the best and to copy them.

But, who *is* the best to learn from? My opinion is that if you want to find the Volunteer Motivator of All Time to emulate, don't look for him (or her) in this century. Instead, you need to go back about 25 centuries—to the time of the Jewish captivity in Babylon and Persia.

I firmly believe that, when confronted with problems, we're wise to seek the solution by looking at Scripture first. My deeply held conviction is that Scripture is sufficient to guide ministry and life, including the issue of motivating and retaining volunteer workers. Where do we find help in the Bible? Rescue comes in the form of a story revealed in the first four chapters of Nehemiah.

You likely know the story: Nehemiah was a Jew born in captivity, sometime around 485-475 B.C. As a servant in Susa, the summer palace for the kings of Persia, he had risen to the prominent position of cupbearer to King Artaxerxes. We don't know how he got there. We know nothing of his previous work experience, but we do know that his current position meant that he was deeply trusted. His job was to taste food before it was given to the king— a step meant to prevent the king from being poisoned. John MacArthur says, "As an escort of the monarch at meals, the cupbearer had a unique opportunity to petition the king. Not only did the king owe him his life since the cupbearer tested all the king's beverages for possible poison, thus putting his own life at risk, but he also became a close confidant."[1]

When his brother, Hanani, came to visit and told Nehemiah of conditions in Jerusalem, God deeply burdened his heart with a desire to provide a solution. Then God miraculously moved the heart of Artaxerxes to allow Nehemiah to go to Jerusalem as governor and to lead the effort to rebuild the city's wall.

In my opinion, Nehemiah's efforts to enlist volunteers for rebuilding the wall, and then his strategy and actions for keeping them when they wanted to quit, make him a shoo-in for Volunteer Motivator of All Time. That's why I will spend the rest of this book looking closely at Nehemiah's work and discussing ways in which we can follow his example today.

Who is this book for? *Anyone who leads volunteers.* However, you will find that I frequently refer to children's ministry, and sometimes to youth ministry. I do this through illustrations, because my life's work has been in children's and youth ministry, and through applications, because a majority of my ministry friends are involved in these areas of ministry as well. I have chosen to add many of their ideas to the manuscript. However, the illustrations and applications are not about the specific ministry *tasks* that the workers do, but about the relationship between the ministry leader and the workers. This mirrors the focus in the biblical passage, which is about the relationship between Nehemiah and his workers, and about what he did for them.

Through this book, you'll have an opportunity to study his techniques and learn to build your own teams more effectively. You will learn how to foster faithfulness in your workers. You will learn how to keep your volunteers from quitting!

Before you go any further, I want you to read chapters 1 through 4 of Nehemiah. Don't skip over this; take the time to get familiar with this story, because it will help you make important application connections later on.

Nehemiah 1

The words of Nehemiah son of Hacaliah: In the month of Kislev in the twentieth year, while I was in the citadel of Susa, Hanani, one of my brothers, came from Judah with some other men, and I questioned them about the Jewish remnant that survived the exile, and also about Jerusalem.

They said to me, "Those who survived the exile and are back in the province are in great trouble and disgrace. The wall of Jerusalem is broken down, and its gates have been burned with fire."

When I heard these things, I sat down and wept. For some days I mourned and fasted and prayed before the God of heaven. Then I said: "O LORD, God of heaven, the great and awesome God, who keeps his covenant of love with those who love him and obey his commands, let your ear be attentive and your eyes open to hear the prayer your servant is praying before you day and night for your servants, the people of Israel. I confess the sins we Israelites, including myself and my father's house, have committed against you. We have acted very wickedly toward you. We have not obeyed the commands, decrees and laws you gave your servant Moses.

"Remember the instruction you gave your servant Moses, saying, 'If you are unfaithful, I will scatter you among the nations, but if you return to me and obey my commands, then even if your exiled people are at the farthest horizon, I will gather them from there and bring them to the place I have chosen as a dwelling for my Name.'

"They are your servants and your people, whom you redeemed by your great strength and your mighty hand. O Lord, let your ear be attentive to the prayer of this your servant and to the prayer of your servants who delight in revering your name. Give your servant success today by granting him favor in the presence of this man."

I was cupbearer to the king.

Nehemiah 2

In the month of Nisan in the twentieth year of King Artaxerxes, when wine was brought for him, I took the wine and gave it to the king. I had not been sad in his presence before; so the king asked me, "Why does your face look so sad when you are not ill? This can be nothing but sadness of heart."

I was very much afraid, but I said to the king, "May the king live forever! Why should my face not look sad when the city where my fathers are buried lies in ruins, and its gates have been destroyed by fire?"

The king said to me, "What is it you want?"

Then I prayed to the God of heaven, and I answered the king, "If it pleases the king and if your servant has found favor in his sight, let him send me to the city in Judah where my fathers are buried so that I can rebuild it."

Then the king, with the queen sitting beside him, asked me, "How long will your journey take, and when will you get back?" It pleased the king to send me; so I set a time.

I also said to him, "If it pleases the king, may I have letters to the governors of Trans-Euphrates, so that they will provide me safe-conduct until I arrive in Judah? And may I have a letter to Asaph, keeper of the king's forest, so he will give me timber to make beams for the gates of the citadel by the temple and for the city wall and for the residence I will occupy?" And because the gracious hand of my God was upon me, the king granted my requests. So I went to the governors of Trans-Euphrates and gave them the king's letters. The king had also sent army officers and cavalry with me.

When Sanballat the Horonite and Tobiah the Ammonite official heard about this, they were very much disturbed that someone had come to promote the welfare of the Israelites.

I went to Jerusalem, and after staying there three days I set out during the night with a few men. I had not told anyone what my God had put in my heart to do for Jerusalem. There were no mounts with me except the one I was riding on.

By night I went out through the Valley Gate toward the Jackal Well and the Dung Gate, examining the walls of Jerusalem, which had been broken down, and its gates, which had been destroyed by fire. Then I moved on toward the Fountain Gate and the King's Pool, but there was not enough room for my mount to get through; so I went up the valley by night, examining the wall. Finally, I turned back and reentered through the Valley Gate. The officials did not know where I had gone or what I was doing, because as yet I had said nothing to the Jews or the priests or nobles or officials or any others who would be doing the work.

Then I said to them, "You see the trouble we are in: Jerusalem lies in ruins, and its gates have been burned with fire. Come, let us rebuild the wall of Jerusalem, and we will no longer be in disgrace." I also told them about the gracious hand of my God upon me and what the king had said to me.

They replied, "Let us start rebuilding." So they began this good work.

But when Sanballat the Horonite, Tobiah the Ammonite official and Geshem the Arab heard about it, they mocked and ridiculed us. "What is this you are doing?" they asked. "Are you rebelling against the king?"

I answered them by saying, "The God of heaven will give us success. We his servants will start rebuilding, but as for you, you have no share in Jerusalem or any claim or historic right to it."

Nehemiah 3

Eliashib the high priest and his fellow priests went to work and rebuilt the Sheep Gate. They dedicated it and set its doors in place, building as far as the Tower of the Hundred, which they dedicated, and as far as the Tower of Hananel. The men of Jericho built the adjoining section, and Zaccur son of Imri built next to them.

The Fish Gate was rebuilt by the sons of Hassenaah. They laid its beams and put its doors and bolts and bars in place. Meremoth son of Uriah, the son of Hakkoz, repaired the next section. Next to him Meshullam son of Berekiah, the son of Meshezabel, made repairs, and next to him Zadok son of Baana also made repairs. The next section was repaired by the men of Tekoa, but their nobles would not put their shoulders to the work under their supervisors.

The Jeshanah Gate was repaired by Joiada son of Paseah and Meshullam son of Besodeiah. They laid its beams and put its doors and bolts and bars in place. Next to them, repairs were made by men from Gibeon and Mizpah—Melatiah of Gibeon and Jadon of Meronoth—places under the authority of the governor of Trans-Euphrates. Uzziel son of Harhaiah, one of the goldsmiths, repaired the next section; and Hananiah, one of the perfume-makers, made repairs next to that. They restored Jerusalem as far as the Broad Wall. Rephaiah son of Hur, ruler of a half-district of Jerusalem, repaired the next section. Adjoining this, Jedaiah son of Harumaph made repairs opposite his house, and Hattush son of Hash-abneiah made repairs next to him. Malkijah son of Harim and Hasshub son of Pahath-Moab repaired another section and the Tower of the Ovens. Shallum son of Hallohesh, ruler of a half-district of Jerusalem, repaired the next section with the help of his daughters.

The Valley Gate was repaired by Hanun and the residents of Zanoah. They rebuilt it and put its doors and bolts and bars in place. They also repaired five hundred yards of the wall as far as the Dung Gate.

The Dung Gate was repaired by Malkijah son of Recab, ruler of the district of Beth Hakkerem. He rebuilt it and put its doors and bolts and bars in place.

The Fountain Gate was repaired by Shallun son of Col-Hozeh, ruler of the district of Mizpah. He rebuilt it, roofing it over and putting its doors and bolts and bars in place. He also repaired the wall of the Pool of Siloam, by the King's Garden, as far as the steps going down from the City of David. Beyond him, Nehemiah son of Azbuk, ruler of a half-district of Beth Zur, made repairs up to a point opposite the tombs of David, as far as the artificial pool and the House of the Heroes.

Next to him, the repairs were made by the Levites under Rehum son of Bani. Beside him, Hashabiah, ruler of half the district of Keilah, carried out repairs for his district. Next to him, the repairs were made by their countrymen under Binnui son of Henadad, ruler of the other half-district of Keilah. Next to him, Ezer son of Jeshua, ruler of Mizpah, repaired another section, from a point facing the ascent to the armory as far as the angle. Next to him, Baruch son of Zabbai zealously repaired another section, from the angle to the entrance of

the house of Eliashib the high priest. Next to him, Meremoth son of Uriah, the son of Hakkoz, repaired another section, from the entrance of Eliashib's house to the end of it.

The repairs next to him were made by the priests from
the surrounding region. Beyond them, Benjamin and Hasshub made repairs in front of their house; and next to them,
Azariah son of Maaseiah, the son of Ananiah, made repairs
beside his house. Next to him, Binnui son of Henadad repaired another section, from Azariah's house to the angle
and the corner, and Palal son of Uzai worked opposite the
angle and the tower projecting from the upper palace near
the court of the guard. Next to him, Pedaiah son of Parosh
and the temple servants living on the hill of Ophel made
repairs up to a point opposite the Water Gate toward the
east and the projecting tower. Next to them, the men of
Tekoa repaired another section, from the great projecting
tower to the wall of Ophel.

Above the Horse Gate, the priests made repairs, each in
front of his own house. Next to them, Zadok son of Immer
made repairs opposite his house. Next to him, Shemaiah son
of Shecaniah, the guard at the East Gate, made repairs. Next
to him, Hananiah son of Shelemiah, and Hanun, the sixth son
of Zalaph, repaired another section. Next to them, Meshullam
son of Berekiah made repairs opposite his living quarters.
Next to him, Malkijah, one of the goldsmiths, made repairs as
far as the house of the temple servants and the merchants,
opposite the Inspection Gate, and as far as the room above
the corner; and between the room above the corner and the
Sheep Gate the goldsmiths and merchants made repairs.

Nehemiah 4

When Sanballat heard that we were rebuilding the wall, he
became angry and was greatly incensed. He ridiculed the
Jews, and in the presence of his associates and the army of
Samaria, he said, "What are those feeble Jews doing? Will

they restore their wall? Will they offer sacrifices? Will they finish in a day? Can they bring the stones back to life from those
heaps of rubble—burned as they are?"

Tobiah the Ammonite, who was at his side, said, "What they
are building—if even a fox climbed up on it, he would break
down their wall of stones!"

Hear us, O our God, for we are despised. Turn their insults
back on their own heads. Give them over as plunder in a land of
captivity. Do not cover up their guilt or blot out their sins from
your sight, for they have thrown insults in the face of the builders.

So we rebuilt the wall till all of it reached half its height, for
the people worked with all their heart.

But when Sanballat, Tobiah, the Arabs, the Ammonites and
the men of Ashdod heard that the repairs to Jerusalem's walls
had gone ahead and that the gaps were being closed, they were
very angry. They all plotted together to come and fight against
Jerusalem and stir up trouble against it. But we prayed to our
God and posted a guard day and night to meet this threat.

Meanwhile, the people in Judah said, "The strength of the
laborers is giving out, and there is so much rubble that we cannot rebuild the wall."

Also our enemies said, "Before they know it or see us, we
will be right there among them and will kill them and put an
end to the work."

Then the Jews who lived near them came and told us ten
times over, "Wherever you turn, they will attack us."

Therefore I stationed some of the people behind the lowest points of the wall at the exposed places, posting them by
families, with their swords, spears and bows. After I looked
things over, I stood up and said to the nobles, the officials and
the rest of the people, "Don't be afraid of them. Remember the
Lord, who is great and awesome, and fight for your brothers,
your sons and your daughters, your wives and your homes."

When our enemies heard that we were aware of their plot
and that God had frustrated it, we all returned to the wall, each
to his own work.

From that day on, half of my men did the work, while the other half were equipped with spears, shields, bows and armor. The officers posted themselves behind all the people of Judah who were building the wall. Those who carried materials did their work with one hand and held a weapon in the other, and each of the builders wore his sword at his side as he worked. But the man who sounded the trumpet stayed with me.

Then I said to the nobles, the officials and the rest of the people, "The work is extensive and spread out, and we are widely separated from each other along the wall. Wherever you hear the sound of the trumpet, join us there. Our God will fight for us!"

So we continued the work with half the men holding spears, from the first light of dawn till the stars came out. At that time I also said to the people, "Have every man and his helper stay inside Jerusalem at night, so they can serve us as guards by night and workmen by day." Neither I nor my brothers nor my men nor the guards with me took off our clothes; each had his weapon, even when he went for water.

May I Pray for You?

Heavenly Father, may the readers of this book find the treatment of Your Word both accurate and insightful. Guide them by Your Holy Spirit to a clear connection between their personal needs and the principles explained here. May You stir their thoughts, impact their hearts, and bless their ministries through the example of Nehemiah. Amen.

Note

1. John MacArthur, *Nehemiah: Experiencing the Good Hand of God* (Nashville, TN: W Publishing Group, 2001), p. 11.

REASONS PEOPLE QUIT

And you think *you've* got it tough . . .

Well, maybe you do. Getting volunteers to serve faithfully in ministry is rarely easy. There's always more ministry to be done than people to do it, and more opportunities than resources. Then there are the critics and bosses (some legitimate, some self-appointed) for what you do—committees, parents, students, pastors, and so forth.

But compared to Nehemiah, you've got it good—*really* good. You'll see.

Before you learn what Nehemiah did to motivate and keep workers, you must appreciate what he faced: intense, increasing opposition; fatigue; loss of vision; discouragement and fear.

Opposition

It's enough to penetrate even the toughest of skins. Words that hurt: false accusations, threats, gossip, mockery. Nehemiah's obstacles started there, but that's no surprise: "When God's people attempt to do God's work in God's way, there will always be opposition."[1]

There certainly was for Nehemiah! As he acted upon his burden to rebuild the wall, the pressure from those who didn't like what he was doing grew. First enemies opposed him, and then even friends. He and his team of volunteers faced ever-increasing challenges from every side—five levels of escalating opposition to completing the work that God had called them to do.

Opposition Level 1: Passive Hostility

When Sanballat the Horonite and Tobiah the Ammonite official heard about this, they were very much disturbed that someone had come to promote the welfare of the Israelites (Neh. 2:10).

Sanballat and Tobiah opposed Nehemiah before work on the wall even began. In fact, Nehemiah was still on his way toward Jerusalem with his entourage when these two adversaries are first mentioned. Who were they, and what was their problem with Nehemiah? Raymond Brown, in his book *The Message of Nehemiah*, gives us some insight:

Sanballat is a Babylonian name meaning "Sin [the moon god] has given life" and probably suggests that his ancestors were among those foreign people who settled in the towns of Samaria to replace the Israelites who had been taken to Assyria in the eighth century . . .

Tobiah was one of Sanballat's close working colleagues, and he too becomes a persistent adversary. His name means "Yahweh is good", and it is generally held that he was another governor from the region probably responsible for the oversight of Ammonite territory.[2]

We're never really told *why* Sanballat and Tobiah didn't want the walls of Jerusalem rebuilt, because that particular detail isn't pertinent to the story. We do know that they were both people of authority and influence—probably governors of regions—so maybe Nehemiah's coming was a threat to them. Whatever their reason was, they didn't like what was going on.

Life in a church today isn't so different. There are usually a couple of people that don't want the new pastor—or the new children's ministry director. Youth pastors may have it toughest, since there's almost *always* somebody that doesn't approve of what *they* do! The reasons behind this kind of immediate opposition may never become apparent—in fact, there may not be any logical reason behind it—but that doesn't necessarily prevent leaders from being affected by it.

That was true of me in my early days of ministry. I secretly hoped—every Sunday morning, I think—that she wouldn't come. Becca was the dominant personality in our youth group, and while she was not openly rebellious, a frigid hostility entered the room with her every week. Her presence intimidated the other teens, throwing cold water on every discussion. She was there because her parents insisted, but everything about her said she didn't want to be a part of what we were doing. There was nothing I did that she liked. Hostility was in her every gesture. Not openly—but you couldn't miss it. Her body language, one-word answers and facial expressions made her attitude very easy to read. As a young youth pastor, my inability to win over Becca made me question my leadership skills, and I even considered quitting. For us tender-skinned types, just the knowledge that someone is opposed to our ministry is enough to discourage us.

Passive opposition also proved to be an obstacle for a pastor friend of mine. He had just been extended an offer to lead a growing, dynamic church. The vote tally of the congregation was about 400 to 6, as I remember. My friend didn't know who the six were who voted against the offer, nor had he been told about any specific concerns. He didn't know if they were hostile toward him in particular or the coming of a new pastor in general, but still he worried about them. What would they do? Were they in leadership? How strongly did they feel? Just the passive opposition of six "no" votes caused him to question whether or not God was leading him to the church. Fortunately, he had the courage to accept the offer despite the possibility of opposition, and God is blessing his ministry there today.

Can you relate? I can certainly identify with how Nehemiah's troubles began—with passive hostility. I admire him very much, because that hostility didn't stop him. But it also didn't *stop*; it quickly escalated into something worse.

Opposition Level 2: Questioning Motives

> But when Sanballat the Horonite, Tobiah the Ammonite
> official and Geshem the Arab heard about it, they mocked
> and ridiculed us. "What is this you are doing?" they asked.
> "Are you rebelling against the king?" (Neh. 2:19).

Suddenly, opposition has morphed into a conspiracy. Geshem
has joined Sanballat and Tobiah in their opposition, and their hostility has changed from passive to active, from non-verbal to verbal. Who was Geshem?

> *Geshem*, or Gashmu as he is called later (6:6, margin) [was]
> an influential Arab who, with his son, "gained control of
> a confederation of Arabian tribes and established their
> rule over a wide territory of North Arabia."[3]

Apparently, Sanballat and Tobiah did not know of the support
Artaxerxes had given to Nehemiah—or if they did, they lied. Without bothering to find out (or else reveal) the truth, they began to
garner support by questioning the reason for Nehemiah's coming.

Isn't that the way people are? When they decide they don't like
you, they assume the worst of motives. "She's just doing this for
herself." "He's just trying to toot his own horn." What's more, they
rarely keep their opinions to themselves. Recently, one Internet
website (supposedly "Christian") promoted some false information about a book written by a close friend of mine. The writer of
the website jumped to a completely false conclusion about the motives and intentions of my friend, and misrepresented and mis-
quoted the content of the book. It has been amazing—and deeply
frustrating—that my friend and others have had to spend extensive
energy mopping up the mess caused by those wrong assumptions.

Anyone in ministry experiences it before too long. Have *you*
wanted to quit because your motives have been questioned? The
slander didn't deter Nehemiah—he just charged ahead. But much
worse opposition was still to come for Nehemiah and his workers.

Opposition Level 3: Enlisting Others

When Sanballat heard that we were rebuilding the wall, he became angry and was greatly incensed. He ridiculed the Jews, and in the presence of his associates and the army of Samaria, he said, "What are those feeble Jews doing? Will they restore their wall? Will they offer sacrifices? Will they finish in a day? Can they bring the stones back to life from those heaps of rubble—burned as they are?" Tobiah the Ammonite, who was at his side, said, "What they are building—if even a fox climbed up on it, he would break down their wall of stones!" (Neh. 4:1-3).

Notice Sanballat's and Tobiah's tactics:

- Name-calling: "feeble Jews"
- Instilling doubt about their purposes: "Will they restore their wall? Will they offer sacrifices?"
- Ridiculing their ability: "Will they finish in a day? Can they bring the stones back to life?"
- Mocking the quality of their work: "If even a fox climbed up on it, he would break down their wall of stones!"

Can you identify? Have you ever had your purpose questioned? Your ability? The quality of your work? When you read the name-calling, mocking and ridiculing of Sanballat and Tobiah, does a face from your past appear in your mind? Have you encountered a Sanballat or a Tobiah? When their modern-day clones appear, our motivation often gets shaken. Many of us are likely to say, "I didn't sign up for this," and look for a way out of whatever commitment we have made.

Notice, too, that Tobiah and Sanballat were intentional about *whom* they made their remarks to: the leadership of the army of Samaria and other officials. Why? They were beginning to organize opposition.

Chuck Swindoll says that Tobiah, however, made a critical mistake:

He claimed that a mere fox "would break their stone wall down." But what they built was not "their" stone wall. The Lord wanted the wall built. He happened to use Nehemiah as the construction superintendent, but God commissioned the work and owned the final product. Carping critics typically look at situations from a human point of view—*their* walls, *their* plans, *their* comfort, *their* procedure, *their* arrangement— usually wrapping their derision in carefully crafted logic or, even worse, cleverly contorted Scripture. They don't stop to think that they may be criticizing God's project.[4]

This, too, has happened to me. My first staff position was interim minister of music at a church in my college town. At 21, I had a lot to learn, and I didn't understand the inner workings of the church. I misunderstood my authority (meaning I thought I had some) and made some changes to what the youth choir was doing. A couple of days later, I got a call from the head deacon, who told me, "Larry, several of the choir parents met together last night . . ." I was hurt that these parents didn't say anything to me first, but instead talked with others. The opposition had organized! They kept the heat on me until—really discouraged—I left the church position just a month or two later.

In Levels One and Two, the opposition targeted Nehemiah. This time, their accusations expanded to include the volunteers he had enlisted to help him. Think about how much more difficult it was becoming for the workers: Their leader was being "shot at," and now they were too. When that happens today, I know it makes volunteers nervous. They like peace, not turmoil. I'm certain the wall-builders in Nehemiah's day were no different.

So far, each new event in Nehemiah's escalating dilemma is something I can relate to. I've had some difficult personal experiences—some caused by me and some not—that are similar to what he faced. But the opposition to the rebuilding of the wall was about to go much further . . .

Opposition Level 4: Enemy Conspiracy

But when Sanballat, Tobiah, the Arabs, the Ammonites and the men of Ashdod heard that the repairs to Jerusalem's walls had gone ahead and that the gaps were being closed, they were very angry. They all plotted together to come and fight against Jerusalem and stir up trouble against it (Neh. 4:7-8).

Few North Americans can identify with this—an enemy that is actively conspiring to *physically* attack us because of our service to God. For Nehemiah, though, this threat was *real*: Ashdod from the west, Samaria (4:2) from the north, the Ammonites from the east, and the Arabs from the south, all conspiring together to attack! Back in verse 3, Nehemiah could have used the "sticks and stones can break my bones . . ." line, but not now—this was getting serious!

In south Asia, Christians are familiar with such threats of violence. Homesteward and Jenny are friends of mine who live in eastern India. They have given their lives to ministering for God, and they face danger in ways we Americans rarely or never do: Their tribe is constantly in conflict with another tribe. Add the dominance of Islam in the region, and my friends face the potential for violent opposition on a daily basis. Homesteward regularly sends Jenny and their young children into the mountains nearby to hide with family members while he continues to minister. In one of the Awana clubs that he works with, a young Muslim girl attended for a while, and then suddenly stopped coming. The club workers found out that *her own father* had killed her, because he feared she would convert to Christianity. In such a hostile environment, Homesteward's life is in constant jeopardy as well, because of his desire to see Muslim children come to Christ. Yet Home, as we call him, never quits—never slows down—in his efforts to spread the gospel to children. Even though the opposition is violent and incredibly dangerous, he is fearless.

Amos (he pronounces it Ah'-mos) is another one of my heroes. He has worked with the poorest of the poor children of India for years. Amos was born into a Hindu family in Nepal, and his family was part of the privileged class (he was a Brahman). He married in his late teens, and his wife's parents were very pleased with the arrangement because of his status. But then Amos found Christ. He was walking along a street one day, and a piece of paper on the ground caught his attention. That piece of paper (we know it as a tract) told him of a God who loved him—a concept so foreign to his Hindu worldview that he was intrigued—and, long story short, Amos found Christ as his Savior. His in-laws were very angry, especially when his wife also became a believer. His own parents disowned him. Then Amos felt called to ministry and decided to go to Bible college. To his in-laws, that was a further betrayal, because now Amos was not only a Christian but also a *poor* one—something they certainly didn't want for their daughter. His passion for Christ led him to focus on the children who lived in the garbage dumps of New Delhi, and as a Bible college student, he began to minister to them. This was another blow to the in-laws: now their daughter's husband was touching the untouchables. Through trickery, they got Amos to bring his wife back home. Once they had her in their home, they forced her into hiding, had the marriage annulled, and then later, so Amos heard, insisted that she marry a Hindu man. Amos never saw her again. He was heartbroken; yet, to this day, he has never stopped working with the children he felt called to serve.

Nehemiah was like that. Opposition didn't dissuade him. Are *you* like that? I don't know if I am or not; I haven't had to face that kind of enemy to my ministry.

So what do you think? Are you beginning to feel like your situation isn't as bad as Nehemiah's? Well, we're not even close to being done describing the obstacles Nehemiah had to face.

Opposition Level 5: Infecting the Inner Circle
Use your imagination a little (or maybe a lot). Suppose you work with fourth-grade boys . . .

One of your best friends comes to you and pleads, "Have you heard the threats? There are people who don't want us working with these kids. If you don't stop teaching that class, you'll get us all killed." (I know, it's hard to imagine this in our world—but humor me.)

Your friend walks away, but then comes back for a second shot. "Please, my friend—stop teaching!! They say they'll kill us all if you don't."

Then a third time: "I beg you—stop serving God. *We're gonna all be dead because of you!*"

Then a fourth time—and a fifth. *Ten times* your friend desperately tries to persuade you to quit.

What would *you* do? If the threat were real, would you continue to teach? Outside opposition is tough, but when pressure comes from the inside, it's almost impossible to ignore.

Homesteward, Jenny and Amos, my friends in India, face opposition from enemies, but they have the support of friends. Some scholars think "the Jews" here might refer to the wives and relatives of the workers on the wall, since many of the workers had come from surrounding villages to live in Jerusalem. Think how disheartening it is to have family and friends echo the message of the enemy! That's exactly what Nehemiah and his workers faced:

> Also our enemies said, "Before they know it or see us, we will be right there among them and will kill them and put an end to the work." Then the Jews who lived near them came and told us ten times over, "Wherever you turn, they will attack us" (Neh. 4:11-12).

That's *real* opposition for Nehemiah. The hostility of the Samarians and Arabs and Ammonites and Ashdodites was a lot, but this time the message came from *Jews*. His *own people*. Friends. Family. People he would have expected to be on his side.

Most of us would quit if facing much less—yet hostility and resistance were not Nehemiah's only headaches.

A Motivational Concern: Getting Past the Mid-point

Evidently, the people in and around Jerusalem got to work quickly, and there was lots of energy in the first days. All the people listed in chapter 3 were organized, energized and jazzed about reconstructing the city's wall. That's pretty clear in Nehemiah 4:6:

> So we rebuilt the wall till all of it reached half its height,
> for the people worked with all their heart.

They worked with *all their heart*! That's pretty commendable, except—wait—the wall was only *half* done. Commendations should wait until the job is finished, and it is apparent as we read on that this mid-point proved to be a crisis point for Nehemiah and his volunteers.

The middle is the most difficult part of nearly any job. After the initial enthusiasm has cooled, and you can't yet see the light at the end of the tunnel, it's just plain tough. It's usually not so difficult to get a group excited about a new project or a new ministry. Lots of people enjoy the freshness of a new idea—a new direction. But by the time you're halfway through, you begin to find out who's really committed and who is not.

Many ministries ask for a seasonal commitment. I've found that, for most churches, the beginning of the school year is a kickoff time for new ministries. And I've also observed that late spring or early summer is usually the time that programs end.

What does this mean for the average church ministry? It means that January and February are critical months. There is mid-point fatigue, holiday fatigue and winter fatigue (at least for those of us in the northern part of the country), all hitting at once. Add the usual cold and flu season, and in children's ministry especially, halfway through the school year is a difficult time.

I've appreciated the impact of Rick Warren's purpose-driven movement, and I have noted in the last few years the number of copy-cat efforts; there are 40 days of this, and 30 days of that. Why aren't there any "200 days of purpose" campaigns? Or even 100 days? Probably because our attention spans aren't that long. Ministry leaders know that it wouldn't fly. Since the wall was half done, and the whole thing was finished in 52 days, I'm guessing that Nehemiah's volunteers had been at it for about 26 days when discouragement hit them. A month of constant work is plenty of time for the newness to have worn off and reality to have set in.

Think about ministry projects you've undertaken. How many of them have been carried to completion? Maybe you're like me: The new ideas I have had greatly exceeded my capacity to finish them. With some projects, I successfully persuade others to join me in starting. But when we get to that mid-way point, I confess that I've often fizzled, and over my years of ministry, so have many of my "great ideas."

Halfway through . . . that's one tough spot! That's where Nehemiah was when the opposition hit the hardest. Are you identifying with him? Does it sound to you like things haven't really changed that much in 2,500 years?

Believe it or not, there were still more obstacles facing Nehemiah.

A Physical Concern: Exhaustion

Meanwhile, the people in Judah said, "The strength of the laborers is giving out" (Neh. 4:10).

The workers were becoming fatigued. Likely, this was no excuse; it was reality. After all, the labor they were undertaking was new to them. According to chapter 3, there were priests, goldsmiths, perfume-makers, rulers, temple servants and merchants involved in building the wall. None of these occupations would have prepared them for moving heavy stones around and putting them back in place. Likely their backs were aching badly, and there were probably cuts, bruises, sprains and blisters all through the ranks. The workers were flat-out *tired*.

The same thing happens in the twenty-first century. People are so *busy* today. I see it in the suburb where I live: dads putting in extra hours to make sure their work gets done so their bosses are happy; single moms working two jobs just to provide for their kids; and then there are the kids' activities. Oh, the activities! There's soccer and dance and karate and Little League and swimming and vacations and movies and going to Grandma's and football and youth theater and shopping and fast food and fixing up our cabin and camping and scouts and teachers' conferences and going to a Cubs game and . . . and . . . and . . . As a result, everyone, it seems, is constantly tired. Nehemiah had an even trickier problem. His people weren't tired because of lesser priorities or the day-to-day busyness of life; they were genuinely exhausted from doing exactly what Nehemiah wanted them to do. They had given it 110 percent for nearly a month. They needed a *break*.

Have you ever tried to motivate tired workers? *Genuinely* tired workers? It's not easy. Nehemiah had that challenge, too. But there is still more.

Spiritual Concerns

There is so much rubble that we cannot rebuild the wall (Neh. 4:10).

Nehemiah's workers, like many today, struggled spiritually as well as physically as the work wore them down. They battled two main issues: their perspective of the work and their assessment of their capacity to get it done.

Lost Perspective: "There Is So Much Rubble . . ."

Was there a lot of rubble still? I think so. I don't think the people in Judah were blowing smoke; I think they were reporting the true situation to Nehemiah. But even if it reflected reality, the comment reveals a deeper problem: Instead of focusing on the half-built wall, the people were looking at the stones still strewn across the hills and valleys near Jerusalem.

A sure sign that motivation for a ministry task is beginning to wane is when people start looking at the problems instead of what they have already been able to do with God's help.

Janet and Wayne were good friends of ours who worked with us in our Awana clubs. One Sunday, our two families went out to dinner together. Janet said, "I want to tell you guys, I think I'm going to quit after this year. I've just had my fill of Awana." As we talked with her further, the issue became clear: It was really about

Susan. Susan was a nearly uncontrollable sixth-grader assigned to Janet's group. She was a piece of work, to say the least. Mature physically for her age, she intimidated the other girls and challenged any authority. Hungry for attention, and trying in all the wrong ways to get it, Susan was rubble to Janet.

I want to pause here to make certain this is clear: There is a difference between *garbage* and *rubble*. Susan was definitely not garbage—garbage is worthless and meant to be thrown away. Rubble is the still un-built wall—unfinished work. Susan clearly was that.

Janet was so frustrated with Susan that she had lost sight of how God had used her with the other girls in her group, and she surely couldn't see how God was even using her with Susan. She was looking at the rubble, not the half-built wall, and was thinking of quitting.

Nehemiah's workers had lost perspective too. Getting it back would be critical to completing the wall.

Focus on Weakness: "We Cannot Rebuild the Wall"

Once again, the people in Judah were only being truthful. However, Nehemiah had never expected them to believe that they could rebuild the wall. *They* couldn't—but God could. In Nehemiah 2:20, he had answered criticism by saying, "the God of heaven will give us success." Nehemiah expected the ability to complete the task to be superhuman, not human. The people had forgotten his words; they were focusing on their own weakness, rather than on the strength of God.

That, by the way, is a great position to be in—to be doing God's work but simultaneously convinced you don't have the strength to do it. Paul says that is when he is strongest:

> But he said to me, "My grace is sufficient for you, for my power is made perfect in weakness." Therefore I will boast all the more gladly about my weaknesses, so that Christ's power may rest on me. That is why, for Christ's sake, I delight in weaknesses, in insults, in hardships, in persecutions, in difficulties. For when I am weak, then I am strong (2 Cor. 12:9-10).

When we can do something in our own strength (though God is the provider even of that), God often is not given the glory. When we can't do what God has put in front of us, His power becomes evident, resulting in greater glory for God.

Most of us have had dark days, and maybe even a dark season, in our lives. My dark season of life began when I contracted Chronic Fatigue Syndrome (CFS) in 1989. I was theoretically entering the prime years of life. But the CFS virus hit me hard—really hard—and deeply altered every part of my life. Certainly, it affected the way I did ministry.

I have vivid memories of Christmas 1989. My son, Ryan, who was 10 at the time, had received a Nintendo set for his birthday earlier in the year. For Christmas, we got him a small computer desk to house the Nintendo system in his room. Of course, the desk needed to be assembled (Dad's job), and I really wanted to do it. I remember lying on the floor of our living room, trying to assemble the desk. My fatigue was so severe that I could only sit up for a minute or two before I had to rest. Over the next six months, my incredible wife, Diane, sometimes wheeled me in a wheelchair because the muscle pain and fatigue were so intense. The fatigue kept me from doing everything myself (as I'd always done because I thought no one could do things as well as I could); I was forced to delegate. My condition made me stop *doing* and start *praying*. It dramatically strengthened my dependence upon God. I suffered for 17 years, and only in the last few has the fatigue finally left. But I don't regret the illness; in fact, I thank God regularly for it. Why? Because of what I learned and how I grew spiritually.

If you have been through some difficult times yourself, you know what I am talking about. During those dark days, God taught me incredible lessons about depending upon Him. I learned things about God that no sermon or Bible study could teach me—things only the deep, shadowy valleys of life could reveal. I learned how much I was trying to do ministry in my own strength, and how little I was depending upon God.

For Nehemiah's workers, it wasn't the challenge of a prolonged and mysterious illness; it was understandable fatigue resulting from hard physical labor. But the effect was the same: They focused upon their own weakness. I know in my dark days I've often said, "I can't do it," and that's exactly what they said.

What do you do? When your workers are ready to give up, how do you turn them around? Nehemiah found the solution—no, God gave it to him. And it resulted in an amazing turn-around—an absolute miracle.

An Incredible Miracle

Think about the Mount Everest-sized motivational task facing Nehemiah:

- The menacing opposition of Sanballat, Tobiah, and the armies they had gathered together
- The threat of a massacre
- The waning interest of the Israelites in a half-done task
- The fatigue of the workers
- The loss of perspective
- The focus on weakness

If I were a leader of a group of volunteers like Nehemiah's—a bunch of laughed-at, worn-out, scared-stiff, glass-half-empty people—here's what I might say: "I need some new blood. There's no life left in these people." "Let's find some fresh troops—these are never going to get it done." "Can you believe how negative these people are? Just let them go. We'll find somebody else to finish the job."

I'm afraid I might also say something like this: "I quit, too."

Nehemiah didn't say any of those things. In fact, he was determined to finish the wall with those people. And he *did*. According to Nehemiah 6:15, they finished the work in 52 days! Not with new blood. No fresh troops. No reinforcements. Nehemiah used the exhausted, weakness-focused, scared-nearly-to-death workers to do it. Is that a miracle, or what? I think it rivals the parting of the Red Sea and the other miracles of the Old Testament. In those instances, God altered the laws of nature, but in this case, it was *human* nature that He overcame, and I think that is every bit as awesome!

I'd like to see some of the best inspirational minds match that today. Give Zig Ziglar, or Tony Robbins, or one of the other motivational gurus that group of workers, and let them see what they could do. I think their contest with Nehemiah would look remarkably similar to Elijah's match with the false prophets on Mount Carmel. Of course, I'm not commenting on their teaching or their relationship with God; I'm just saying that God's Old Testament man, led by the spirit of God, would win—and win big. Hands down, Nehemiah would win any contest of motivators. In my opinion, he is, without question, the motivational guru of all time.

Would you like to learn Nehemiah's secrets for bringing about such a change in his workers? Call this number within 24 hours, and in 6 easy payments you can . . . I'm kidding, I'm kidding!

Nehemiah did seven incredibly wise things, by the leading of God. In fact, I am so persuaded of their effectiveness, I want to make a prediction: If you implement these seven principles consistently, you will transform the way your people respond to ministry.

We'll talk about each of the seven principles in the following chapters. We'll also travel back in time to reflect on Nehemiah's motivational leadership—and the sometimes thrilling, sometimes overwhelming process of rebuilding Jerusalem's wall—through the eyes of one of the Israelite workers: Uzziel the goldsmith.

Think and Talk About It

1. Review the obstacles that Nehemiah faced. Can you name them in order, and understand why they increased in difficulty?

2. What kind of a person do you think Nehemiah was?

3. What was the "ministry task" Nehemiah undertook, and how is it similar to yours?

4. Which of Nehemiah's obstacles do you feel were the most challenging? Why?

5. Have you ever seen a "Sanballat" or a "Tobiah" in action? What happened (be careful not to betray confidences)?

6. Look at the workers around you. Which obstacles do you feel are the greatest issues for them?

7. Without looking ahead to how Nehemiah resolves his difficult situation, are there things you already admire about him from the text? What are they?

Notes

1. John MacArthur, *Nehemiah: Experiencing the Good Hand of God* (Nashville, TN: W Publishing Group, 2001), p. 38.
2. Raymond Brown, *The Message of Nehemiah* (Downers Grove, IL: InterVarsity Press, 1998), pp. 60-61.
3. Ibid., p. 61.
4. Charles Swindoll, *Hand Me Another Brick* (Nashville, TN: W Publishing Group, 2006), p. 69.

MOTIVATION 1

FIRST RESPONSE

Let me set this stone down before I introduce myself … there. Whew! That's a heavy one!

I'm Uzziel, a goldsmith. You may have read my name before, but you likely didn't remember it—maybe you didn't even notice it. Nehemiah recorded my name in his account of the building of the wall. I didn't get much press—just my name mentioned. But that's fine with me, because the story isn't about me. It's about how God incredibly used Nehemiah to lead us to do something we should have done years earlier: remove the disgrace from Jerusalem by rebuilding the wall.

I'd like to tell you how the whole thing started for me. I was in a pretty comfortable spot in life when Nehemiah came to town. My father, Harhaiah, had been a goldsmith before me, and a pretty good one, too. In fact, he built quite a reputation for our family. From the time I was about six, he taught me about crafting gold into fine articles—rings, necklaces, and such. In recent years, traders traveled constantly through the city of Jerusalem, so my business always had new customers coming and going.

My father was one of the fortunate ones who didn't get taken captive. Sixty years earlier, Nebuchadnezzar destroyed Jerusalem, plundered the temple, and took a thousand craftsmen captive to Babylon. Because Dad was just a teenager at the time, I guess the Babylonians didn't think that he could be a skilled craftsman (but he was, because my grandfather had trained him), and they left him here in Jerusalem.

For a lot of years, the country was so poor that there was little gold to smith, and I remember, when I was little, often hearing my dad worry about where we would get food to eat. In those lean times, Dad still worked hard to maintain his goldsmithing skills, and he involved me in his work, too. He would say, "Uzziel, some day business will be better, and I want you to be ready so you can provide for your family." He would take a small lump of gold and melt it. We would make it into a ring, then melt it down again, and make it into a small pendant, and then into something else—just to stay in practice.

I guess it was because of how poor we were for so long that I never thought much about the broken-down walls here in Jerusalem. Not until Nehemiah came, anyway. I first heard about the curious visitors from my neighbors. They said, "Did you see the horses and soldiers in town? We hear they are from Susa, the Persian capital." We wondered why they were here, and who brought them—and then the elders of the city asked me to come to a meeting.

Nehemiah immediately impressed me. As he told how he had heard of the condition of Jerusalem, and how God had led him to come to help, I right away sensed he was a man of God. As he told of the trip from Susa, I couldn't help thinking, *This is miraculous; this is God leading him*. Then I noticed how he prayed; it seemed so natural—so real. It was like he really believed he was talking to the Lord! You know, I think it was the sense of this man's closeness to our God that persuaded me so quickly.

To be honest, I was a little embarrassed—and a little mad at myself—that I hadn't seen the broken-down walls as a disgrace to God. I have to admit, that's exactly what they have been. I've personally heard travelers laughing at us, saying things like, "If your God is so great, He certainly isn't protecting you very well." I remember one time several Philistines were here trading, and one of them went over and pushed on one of the stones that were still part of a remnant of the wall. The stone fell from its perch and tumbled farther down the hill. "Strong wall you have here," he mocked. His companions, I remember, nearly doubled over in laughter. None of us Jews were laughing, though.

Like I said, I was embarrassed to have this disgrace pointed out to us. Yet if it took the Lord sending this man 500 miles to help us see it and fix it, I was ready to listen.

When Nehemiah said, "Let's rise up and build," my heart was stirred—deeply, deeply stirred. And I found myself at the front of the group, volunteering to help rebuild the wall.

"You're going to do *what*?" was my wife's response when I told her. "What about your hands?" I knew what her concern was: Goldsmith work takes delicate, sensitive fingers. And I was going to be handling stones—lots of stones. That really required tough hands and calloused fingers, not hands like mine. Mine would get that mortar stuff on them, too, and they would get raw, sore and blistered. But it didn't matter. "My hands will be okay," I assured my wife. But in my heart I hoped that it wouldn't take too long for them to heal afterward.

So that's why I'm here. Why my hands look the way they do. Yep—and why my arms and back are so sore. This is a lot more strenuous than making jewelry and coins!

I believe God has brought Nehemiah here to lead this important work, and I'm proud to be part of it. We're only four days into this project, and we have made some real progress. We'll see how long it will take, but as of right now, I'm in this until it is finished.

Your First Response

Managing your first response when something unexpected happens can be quite a challenge! Your people will be watching, and how you react to obstacles or opportunities will have a significant effect on how they accept your leadership. How *you* adapt to change and uncertainty will affect how they function as a team. Do you often panic? They might as well. Do you complain? Expect the same from them. Do you lose your cool? They will withdraw from you.

The first response in the face of a crisis tells so much about a leader. We learn a lot about Nehemiah's character in observing how he responded to a crisis. But before we look at him, consider how you might respond to each of the following scenarios.

Marianne, your best Sunday morning worker: "I'm sorry, but I can't teach the fourth-graders anymore. My husband has made the decision to leave the church." If you were the children's director hearing that, what would be your first response?

Tom, your senior pastor: "The elders had a meeting last night about your ministry. They had some questions about the direction in which you are taking it. I think that they are okay for now, but we'll have to talk later." If you were the children's pastor, what would be your first response?

Gretchen, a ministry friend: "Our group is planning a youth group trip to Italy. We think you are the perfect one to lead it, but it will take three weeks. Would you consider it?" If you were a youth pastor, what would be your first response?

You walk behind two church members, and you overhear them talking about the recent children's choir concert: "Were you here for that children's choir concert? It was the lamest we've ever had."

"Yes, I was. Could you believe how unprepared the children were? We need a new director." If you were that children's choir director, what would be your first response?

A Personal Illustration

"Dad's in the hospital—you may need to come home." My brother Richard's phone call shattered our plans for the week. Diane and

I learned that Dad had not been feeling well for a few weeks, and then finally went to the doctor when he didn't improve. Cattle ranchers don't go to the doctor for just any little ailment, so I knew that something serious was wrong.

"We'll be ready to come—just keep us posted." A day or two later, Richard called back, and the news was really bad: Our father had acute leukemia, and he didn't have long to live. Richard said we needed to get there fast. We were living in southern California, and it was at least a day's trip to get to central Nebraska—first the plane flight to Denver, then an Amtrak train to the town of Kearney, where my dad was in the hospital.

We made it in time for me to get to talk to Dad a little in the afternoon. He was pretty heavily drugged and only said, "Well, Larry's here." I could tell he was pleasantly surprised to see me. I held his hand for a while, and then he went back to sleep and we left to get a room at a nearby hotel.

At about midnight, the phone in the hotel room rang. "You'd better come now," the nurse from the hospital said. I dressed as fast as I could and rushed to the hospital's ICU waiting room. Richard (a rancher like Dad) and our sister, Caroline (a pastor's wife), joined me, and we waited with our mom for news of our dad's condition.

Then the doctor emerged through those swinging stainless steel doors that separated the ICU from the rest of the hospital. He had probably done this dozens of times, and he knew exactly how to handle it. He looked down, shook his head, and said just two words: "I'm sorry." We didn't need to hear any more to know that the father we deeply loved and respected was gone.

Every family experiences moments like these: receiving news of the impending death of a loved one, gathering together at the hospital, and then being told that it's over. But something happened that night in that little hospital that I believe rarely happens. It wasn't the disease—or the news—or the doctor's kind manner. It was my mother's response to the doctor's words.

Mom and Dad had lived all of their adult lives on a cattle ranch. There were no separate jobs, no separate groups of friends. Their lives were entirely intertwined during their 42 years of marriage—

they were best friends; deeply in love; and partners in business, in ministry and in *life*. Mom lost so much when the doctor's two words were spoken.

You'd think she would cry. *I* did. Richard and Caroline did. I consider that a pretty normal response. But Mom did something better, and I'll never forget it.

Mom bowed her head and began to *pray*. Can you believe it? At the shock of the news that her husband had died, she didn't cry. She *prayed*. It wasn't just any prayer, either; she *praised* God—for their happy marriage, for their love, for all the good times they had shared, that Dad was in heaven, and for his godly example to all of us. Do you get it? Her *automatic reaction* to hearing that her life partner was gone was to *pray*. Her tears came later, but her *first* response to this crisis was to *pray*.

That kind of spiritual maturity is rare—very rare. But it exists in my mother. And 2,500 years ago, it existed in Nehemiah.

Nehemiah's First Response

Most of us, though we might struggle to have this first response ourselves, can easily recognize the need to pray for God's strength, comfort and guidance when we are faced with devastating news. We might have more trouble remembering that prayer should be our first response in other circumstances as well. Nehemiah models for us a consistent commitment to come before God whenever he reaches a point in his journey where a decision must be made. The Bible reveals three very different instances in which Nehemiah responded with prayer to God.

Nehemiah Prayed First When There Was Bad News

In chapter 1, Nehemiah's first response when he heard the news from Jerusalem was to pray (1:4). He was so overwhelmed by the bad report that he *mourned and fasted and prayed*. If you haven't studied his prayer, do so. It's so different from the one I might offer— I'd probably pray, "Lord, help those poor people!" But Nehemiah's prayer is one of confession on his people's behalf and petition for success on what he was about to attempt. Pretty amazing first response, wouldn't you say?

Nehemiah Prayed First When There Was a Ministry Opportunity

Then, in chapter 2, his first response to an open door was to pray in the middle of his conversation with King Artaxerxes:

> In the month of Nisan in the twentieth year of King Artaxerxes, when wine was brought for him, I took the wine and gave it to the king. I had not been sad in his presence before; so the king asked me, "Why does your face look so sad when you are not ill? This can be nothing but sadness of heart."
>
> I was very much afraid, but I said to the king, "May the king live forever! Why should my face not look sad when the city where my fathers are buried lies in ruins, and its gates have been destroyed by fire?"
>
> The king said to me, "What is it you want?"
>
> Then *I prayed to the God of heaven*, and I answered the king, "If it pleases the king and if your servant has found favor in his sight, let him send me to the city in Judah where my fathers are buried so that I can rebuild it" (Neh. 2:1-5, emphasis added).

I can imagine Nehemiah praying, "Okay, God, this is it. You've opened the door for me—now help me answer the king in the right way."

Nehemiah Prayed First When There Was Opposition

Later, Nehemiah faced the conspiracy of Sanballat, the mocking by Tobiah, and the threat from the army of Samaria. Again Nehemiah's response was to *pray* (4:4,9). Not first to defend against the threat, or to respond to the mocking (probably what I would do), but first to pray.

Whether it's distressing news, an open door or opposition, Nehemiah first addressed situations with prayer.

Why would a person pray *first*?

Our first response usually reveals our heart. Have you ever snapped at your spouse or at your kids? That was your heart showing. Sometimes, our hearts can be pretty ugly (the Bible has something to say about that in Jeremiah 17:9[1]). Mine certainly can be. Before my head takes over and common sense prevails, my first response can sometimes embarrass, offend and even injure. That's why, when my first response is more godly, I quietly breathe a sigh of relief: *Good—I didn't blow that one.*

What Praying Does and Doesn't Do

I confess. I've been inwardly disappointed in the past because God didn't respond to my prayers the way I thought He should. Can you identify with that? I've also observed that when I have wrong expectations for prayer, I am less likely to pray as a first response. If I think prayer should accomplish things it's not meant to accomplish, then I can become frustrated or discouraged in prayer when those things don't happen. I have found it helpful to think through the purpose of prayer so I don't miss out on the important work that God wants to do in and through me as I pray. Think about what prayer does and doesn't do:

Praying Isn't for God

It doesn't get His attention. It's not like God needs us to make Him aware of a need or a situation. He doesn't daydream. He hasn't forgotten. If God is omniscient, there is nothing we can say to make Him more alert—more tuned in to what is going on.

It doesn't help Him understand what is needed. It's not like our opinion will give Him a more complete perspective, or help Him make better sense of what the situation is.

It doesn't provide comfort for Him or cure His loneliness. God doesn't need our prayers to help Him feel like He's not alone. If He is the all-sufficient one, He has no needs.

Praying Is for People

First, it is for the person praying. It cements our dependence upon God. When we bring our concerns to God, it's pretty hard to ignore the fact that He may be involved in both the reasons for the concern and any potential resolution to the situation. When prayer is our first response, it means that we are in a God-dependent position at the beginning, and that is one great place to start. Praying first also will keep us from making decisions—or even comments—rashly. Chuck Swindoll says, "Prayer *makes me wait*. I cannot pray and work at the same time. I have to wait to act until I finish praying. Prayer forces me to leave the situation with God; it makes me wait."[2]

Second, it is for others. It reminds them of who is really in control and bolsters their faith that God is involved in their situation. It is comforting to others to know someone is praying for them. They sense how much that person cares, and it motivates them to keep moving forward.

Prayer
isn't for God;
prayer
is for people.

I can tell you from personal experience that prayer is an effective first tool to use to help people stay faithful in ministry. In the years when my wife, Diane, and I served the Los Angeles area as missionaries in children's ministry, we received financial support from our home church. It was the practice of our pastor, Bob Carpenter, to pray each week for a different missionary that was supported by the church. I confess that way too often I daydreamed during his prayer, *but never when he was praying for me*. I could tell, too, that he was interested in our ministry by how he prayed. Pastor Bob prayed for details, which told me he had taken the time to know what was going on and what our needs were. Need I add that his prayers *for* us were encouraging *to* us?

How Does Prayer Become a Motivating Tool?

Your commitment, as a leader, to cultivating the habit of prayer as a first response brings with it a number of benefits for your workers and the ministry you're doing together. Not only do you set a godly example for others to follow, but you also have opportunities to encourage and energize your team members in profound ways.

Your Workers Need to Know That Prayer Is Your First Response

You'll need to live this out in front of them, won't you? Get in the habit of praying as your first response. Prayer can begin a meeting, but it should also begin a conversation.

Scenario #1

Suppose Jeremy, one of your volunteers, comes to you visibly upset. "I've got to talk to you about Trevor," he begins. His face is flushed, and his breathing is fast.

Think about how you might respond. Now think about how things might go if you respond like this: "Okay, Jeremy, but before you tell me what is going on, let's ask for God's discernment." Then you pray:

"Heavenly Father, Jeremy's come to discuss a situation with me right now, and we both need Your peace and Your discernment. Help us to be wise in our conversation as we seek to understand what is going on here and how we should proceed. Give us Your wisdom and Your words. In Jesus' name, Amen."

What does the prayer do? It calls on God's power for the things you will need in order to give good advice: peace, discernment and wisdom. It also gives Jeremy time to compose himself. It helps him regain a God-perspective of the situation—and reminds him that God will be part of this conversation—before you start to talk.

Scenario #2

Lindsay catches you after the Sunday morning service. "I feel God was speaking directly to me during the pastor's sermon this morning. I have been thinking about starting a small group for special-needs kids—you remember that my niece is one—in our Sunday School, and this morning, what he said just convicted me that it is exactly what we should do. Will you help me?"

Lindsay isn't thinking about the fact that the rooms are all taken, the budget has been cut, and you can't get enough help for Sunday School as it is—but those things sure come to your mind immediately. How do you respond? Rather than throw cold water on her enthusiasm—or give her free rein to do her own thing—*start* with prayer:

"Lord, help Lindsay to know clearly what it is You are laying upon her heart. Provide a room and funds, and give her people to share her vision—people who are not already overworked in ministry. Give me wisdom about how best to help her. In Your name, Amen."

Train yourself: *react* with prayer to burdens, to open doors, to opposition and to challenges. You will see. God will use this practice to bless your leadership.

Your Workers Need to Know You Are Praying for Them

It should go without saying that you pray for your volunteers. But do they know it? Here's an idea: The founder of Awana, Art Rorheim, has for years created a prayer chart annually. On this chart, he lists missionaries, co-workers and others he wants to remember to pray for. It's actually a booklet of names with boxes next to them. As he faithfully prays for each one, he checks off the boxes by his or her name. Can you imagine the encouragement first to see his book, and then to find your name in it, and finally to see a bunch of check marks by your name?

If you are a list-keeper, this is a great one for you. Do what Art does: Make a list of your workers that you want to pray for, and then hold yourself accountable to pray for them regularly. When you do, check off their names so you know you've remembered. Don't be afraid to let them know of your list and that you have prayed for them. Just knowing you have systematically remembered them in prayer will be refreshing for them.

Your Workers Need to Hear You Praying for Them

Go into a classroom, get the students' attention, and then say, "Let's thank God together for your teacher." Lead the students in prayer, praising Him for the teacher's commitment, for his/her giftedness, etc. Or ask one of the students to do the same. You will not only bless the teacher, but you will also help the students learn to be a blessing.

Alternatively, pray with your volunteers privately (some will be more comfortable with this approach). Thank God for their willingness to serve. Be sincere—after all, isn't God the source of our giftedness, our faithfulness? Isn't it proper to thank Him for developing those things in others?

Now, go back to the illustrations on page 40. What if your first response to each of these was to pray?

Think and Talk About It

1. Review the circumstances presented in this chapter in which Nehemiah responded with prayer.
2. Do his circumstances make you think of any recent situations you have found yourself in?
3. Who has greatly encouraged you through prayer?
4. What do you think of Fowler's comments, "Prayer isn't for God" and "Prayer is for people"?
5. Do you think you motivate others by praying for them? Could you motivate them in this way?
6. Think through your ministry schedule. When is prayer a part of it? Maybe a better way to ask this is: When do you pray with your workers or your students?
7. When *could* you make prayer a bigger part of your ministry?
8. What is your life pattern with regard to praying first? Is this something you could improve upon? What would be a way you could begin to remind yourself to do it?

Notes
1. "The heart is deceitful above all things and beyond cure. Who can understand it?" (Jer. 17:9).
2. Charles R. Swindoll, *Hand Me Another Brick* (Nashville, TN: W Publishing Group, 2006), p. 33.

FAMILIES INVOLVED TOGETHER

Therefore I stationed some of the people behind the lowest points of the wall at the exposed places, posting them by families, with their swords, spears and bows.
NEHEMIAH 4:13

Uzziel here again.

I guess you're aware that we are almost four weeks into our project, and there has been huge turmoil among the workers. You've probably heard what the Arabs and the Ammonites are plotting—they're threatening to attack us.

The first couple of weeks were amazing; I alternated picking up rocks, shaping logs into rollers to move the large stones, rolling the stones to the wall, and fitting them into place. I especially enjoyed the last, because it was like solving a puzzle for me. During those first days, sleep didn't matter a whole lot; adrenaline kept us going. The men next to me and I worked as long as we could after dark, and we were back at it before the sun came up each morning.

But then the rumors started. At first, it didn't bother any of us, but when the talk about planned attacks persisted, we began to think—no, to worry—about it. I think we worried a little at first, but then I began (I can't speak for the others) to worry a lot. We weren't sure what was true and what wasn't. Was the Samarian army advancing on Jerusalem? We heard that rumor. What about the Arabs and the Ammonites? Were they on their way to attack?

I'm working on the west side of the wall, and I'm thinking even if the Arabs and Ammonites do attack, they probably won't start here since they would come from the east. The Old Gate is just east of here, and this is the least accessible part of the wall. I confess I have worried some about the Ashdodites; they are part of the conspiracy as well, and they might attack here since they would come from the west.

My greatest concern, though, is about the southeast part of the city. I moved my family there several years ago, when business began to increase in Jerusalem. Our house is located just off the trade route. I picked the spot on purpose because it was a good location for business, but now I think, *It's an awful location if the armies come from the east.* I can't help thinking as I pick up stones (actually, I think about it with every single stone I pick up), I wish this stone was protecting my three little sons. I haven't heard how the wall is coming over there. I sure hope the workers there are doing a good job …

Then I worry about my elderly dad, Harhaiah. He's in his 70s now and has a bad back. He didn't want to be left out of the work, so I know he is doing what he can. But I've lost track of where he is. I wish I knew, because if I did, I'd try to get him here by me. I also think a lot about my brothers and cousins. *A lot.* In fact, I think too much about them. The worry is keeping me from doing my best.

Now, look at this hillside over there. I've been picking up rocks for more than 25 days now, and there are still so *many* left. Just looking, you can't tell I've picked up any at all. And my hands . . . look at them. They're starting to callous over, but they've never looked this messed up. It will be a long time until I can craft a delicate ring again. All of this is really starting to get to me. I haven't told anyone, but I secretly want to just quit and go back home.

"Uzziel? Uzziel? Are you there?"

Sorry to interrupt my conversation with you, but some-one's calling me . . .

Praise the Lord, praise the Lord Almighty! You'd think God just heard my prayer and answered it immediately! Do you know who that was? Do you *know* who that was? Nehemiah! Yes, Nehemiah himself. In the flesh!

And do you know what he wants me to *do*? Do you know what he wants me to do? Go work on the wall right by my home! Waaaaaahoooooo! Can you believe it? The very thing I was longing for, Nehemiah just told me to do! Except I'm to do one thing first: find my brothers and my father and have them join me. Can you believe it? Can you believe it? I'm on my way! I don't even care that I'll be working in a more dan-gerous area now. At least I'll be able to look out for my family.

The principle Nehemiah understood and implemented 2,500 years ago still holds true today: The more the family is together, the higher the motivation is to stay involved.

Families Involved Together

Where do we see this philosophy lived out today? Think about the families you know. Which ones have whole family involvement in an activity or hobby? I'm sure you know soccer families, or camp-ing families, or boating families, or . . . you get the idea. I enjoy running, and one family has caught my attention at several of the local 5K races that I've participated in. Mom, Dad and four kids, currently between 7 and 12 years old, *all* run. I don't know them personally, but it's pretty easy to see that their family identity is tied closely to the activity they participate in together.

It's not usually that way at church. Even when several family members are active in ministry, they're usually involved in different ministries. Let me propose something better: families involved together in ministry.

There are many benefits to this approach to serving God as families.

Getting Families Involved Together Increases Commitment

My ministry, Awana, enjoys a high level of loyalty on the part of many families—because the whole family gets involved. Dad and Mom are both leaders, often in groups with or near their own children. Generally, they can be counted on to stay put as a family unit. I believe their connection together in ministry is a strong element in keeping them faithful.

Becky Blaine, from Missouri, told me the following:

> My husband was involved in music ministry, and I was involved in children's ministry. It became difficult to serve because we were both in different ministries. So he stepped back from music and joined me in children's ministry in order for us to work together as a family. It was good for our relationship, because it is not my ministry anymore but ours. Now our girls see us preparing and serving together. It has become very healthy for our family.

Many moms, dads, grandpas and grandmas serve in the children's department while their kids are little; in fact, parents tend to follow their children up through the programs, volunteering where their kids are. I have to confess that I have been frustrated in the past because so many parents moved on in this way. I thought, *Do they only care about their own children? Can't they have enough heart for the others that they stay and work even when their kids aren't in the group?* As I've grown older (and wiser), I understand more that such a model is good, except . . . it generally trails off in middle school. Here's what I've observed about volunteers at different levels:

	Moms' Involvement	Dads' Involvement
Nursery	Some moms prefer to let others work with their babies; they're just too tired.	Dads stay away in droves: "What—change the diapers of a kid that's not my own?"
Pre-school	Moms really like to volunteer; many are highly involved.	On occasion, dads help, but only a small minority; it's primarily a women's world.
Early Elementary	The "teacher" moms stay involved; volunteerism is still high.	Dads feel a little more comfortable, so male involvement increases a little.
Middle Elementary	Same as Early Elementary	This is many dads' sweet spot; if you're going to recruit dads, this is the easiest group.
Middle School	Group dynamics change, and program structure changes. Both of these factors mean that many parents stop volunteering in their kids' groups. Child-to-volunteer ratios increase so fewer parents are needed (or wanted).	
Senior High	More program structure changes; the most-sought-after youth workers are young adults, not parents. Most parents feel unwanted and further estranged from the activities of their teenagers.	

The sad fact is that in most churches, there is no easy way for parents to stay involved with their children—whether helping with programs in which their kids participate, or serving together with their children in family-friendly ministry opportunities. A few—but it is too many—youth pastors simply don't want the parents as leaders: They say it is "disruptive" and that the kids won't open up if their parents are in the room. While these youth leaders' concerns may be valid in a lot of cases, there are other solutions. There also are few opportunities for parents and their teenage children to serve together. It's true that creating these opportunities takes work: Church leaders must coordinate their program planning efforts, adjust normal patterns of recruitment, and maybe even change their philosophies. I maintain that it is well worth the effort to encourage families to minister together.

As an author and frequent conference speaker, it is quite difficult for me to volunteer regularly in my own church. However, I stay committed to serving God in it, and in Awana clubs in particular, since that is the ministry organization to which God has called me. Being there regularly is a challenge with my travel schedule, but the last few years I've made it a high priority; in fact, I rarely missed a meeting, and neither did Diane. I made sure that even when there were "big" opportunities, my travel fit around my volunteer ministry, Awana. Why? Our grandchildren were in the ministry with us. Then our oldest grandson, Tyler, when he turned 13, became a "junior leader" with us. I didn't want to miss because I didn't want him to miss. Do you see? My commitment to be there regularly deepened considerably simply because I had my grandkids and my wife in the same ministry with me.

Mel Jones, a mom from Nebraska whose family is involved in ministry together, wrote this to me:

> My family all serves in Awana this year. This makes Wednesday nights a huge deal for our family every week. It has improved my kids' attendance tremendously. They haven't missed a single night since we all serve together now. It has increased my passion to serve in children's ministries. My husband has even talked about going into full-time ministry because of the growth that we've seen. The dedication I see from my older kids to be there for the little ones is so heart warming . . . I know it's God working in our lives.

The obvious truth is this: *You are going to be much more invested—and therefore much less likely to quit—when you are serving next to a family member.* Think about it: If you have committed to a ministry along with your spouse—or with your son or daughter, or another family member—you will naturally be much more hesitant to walk away from your team and the work you're doing together.

Getting Families Involved Together Increases Spiritual Conversation at Home

Families—especially dads and kids—talk about what they have in common. If what they have in common is soccer, that's what they will talk about. If it's hiking, vacations, hobbies, their favorite sports team—whatever—it gives them a basis for conversation.

Many dads have confessed to me that leading their families spiritually is hard for them. I believe one reason is that the spiritual lives in most Christian families today are compartmentalized.

I'm sure you've had conversations in your home like this one between Katie and Tamara (Katie's the mom):

> **Katie:** "How was your day at school?"
> **Tamara:** "Fine."
> **Katie:** "Did your math teacher give you a test?"
> **Tamara:** "Nope."
> **Katie** (trying to deepen the conversation): "Did anything exciting happen at school?"
> **Tamara:** "Huh-uh."
> **Katie:** "What did you and your friends do during lunch?"
> **Tamara:** "Just talked."

Katie wasn't able to pry more than one or two words at a time out of her daughter. Later, she timed Tamara's telephone conversation with a classmate and noted that it lasted for 45 minutes. She wondered, "Why can't she talk to me that long about school?"

Here's why (at least, here's part of the reason): Tamara has school activities in common with her classmate, but not with her mom. School compartmentalizes life, as do many other things.

That's the way life is. When parents are not in a certain compart-ment in their child's life, conversation takes extra effort on both sides. Conversations are al-most *always* harder when they don't involve a common in-terest or activity.

That's why spiritual con-versations are often so hard for families. What are they going to talk about? In a typ-ical church, family members of different ages don't attend the same classes; kids aren't with their parents in the worship service; and often youth and adult fellowship times are even separate.

> Spiritual conversations are often hard for families because they have no spiritual activities in common.

Being a guy, I know how this is especially helpful for dads to un-derstand. You ladies are pretty good at heart-to-heart talks, but we guys generally need an activity to build conversation around. So when families serve God together in a ministry, dads have a founda-tion—common ground—for talking with their kids about spiritual matters. Now, obviously we parents can't stay completely involved in everything our kids do, or they will never grow up, but that doesn't mean we can't find certain meaningful activities to do (and talk about) together.

Trevor Lambert, a ministry friend from Kentucky, says this:

> Serving together [as a family] is a blessing. We can go home and share about how things went that night and what went right or wrong or improve discipline next week. Just talking and sharing has a positive impact on my family.

Jason was a young dad who had grown up in an outright-pagan family and found Christ as a teenager. As a result, he didn't have any personal experience with how godly parents (especially dads) func-tioned. He confessed to me, "I really don't know how to talk to my kids about spiritual things." I encouraged him to just tell his young kids what God was teaching him. "I have been," he answered, "but I feel like it's not very natural."

I asked him, "So what *do* you talk about with your kids?"

"My son is seven, and he's already a Cubs fanatic, so we talk about the players a lot. And I play video games, so we talk about them. And soccer—he started playing that this year, so we talk about it."

I interpreted his response: "In other words, you talk about the activities that you have in common."

"Yeah, I guess," he answered.

"So what spiritual activities do you share with him?"

"None, I guess." Jason squirmed a little. "But I make sure he's in Sunday school and church."

"Let me suggest what will help you the most at home: Get involved in a ministry that your son is involved in, and then you will have something in common to talk about."

Jason took my advice and began working as a club leader in his son's group. He later shared with me how much he was enjoying it. "What has it done to your conversations at home?" I asked, remembering our earlier discussion.

He paused for a few seconds and then brightened. "I remember what you said about sharing activities together, and you know—wow—it *has* changed the way we talk together. We talk as much about club now as we do about the Cubs! We have a way to go, though, before our spiritual conversations pass up our conversations about video games." We both laughed, but I felt really good inside that Jason had gotten it—joint involvement provides a basis for conversations at home.

Whether it is serving in your child's ministry, or serving alongside your spouse or older kids, you will find that being involved together will have a positive, dramatic effect on your home conversations.

Getting Families Involved Together Improves Discipleship

You've probably heard the verse, "Train a child in the way he should go, and when he is old he will not turn from it" (Prov. 22:6).

Most people focus on the promise at the end of the verse; some wonder if it is a promise or a general principle. Others discuss what "in the way he should go" really means. But too often we overlook the first word—"train." Is that what happens at church? In your Sunday school or youth group?

What *is* training? I've heard it described this way:

1. I will do it; you watch.
2. We do it together.
3. You try it; I will watch.
4. You do it alone.
5. You do it; someone else watches.

Think about how this applies to the life-development of a child:

The training step	The life-development principle	A real-life example of families involved together
I will do it; you watch.	When children are young, they see their parent or parents work in the ministry they are involved in.	Chris and Jennifer loved music, and they decided to start a children's choir in their church when their daughter, Amy, was just three. Of course, Amy was excited to be involved because Mom and Dad were excited themselves.
We do it together.	When children get to middle elementary age, they begin to participate with their parents in ministry.	Amy had started piano lessons at age seven, and at nine she wanted to play the keyboard along with the children's choir. Of course, Mom and Dad said yes, and although Amy wasn't too good at first, she improved quickly because she was so motivated.
You try it; I will watch.	When kids become adolescents, they can take lots of responsibility—under the careful eye of a mentor.	Amy had outgrown children's choir, and there was no music ministry in the Junior High group. "Why don't you put together a girls' group from among your friends?" Chris challenged her. "You know a lot about what to do from watching us, and I'll help you if you get stuck."

The training step	The life-development principle	A real-life example of families involved together
You do it alone.	When our children become young adults, they serve God apart from the urging or supervision of their parents.	Amy went to college and attended a small church in her college town. Seeing there was no children's choir in the church, she asked the pastor if she could start one. He was supportive, and for nearly four years, Amy developed her skills in ministry in that little church.
You do it; someone else watches.	When our children become parents, they will begin the process of discipling in ministry over again with their children.	Amy met her husband at college, and after they married, moved and started a family, she observed the children's worship at her new church and immediately knew something had to be done: "I will develop a worship team to lead these kids." She did it, and her children began to observe their mother serving.

Music may not be the thing for your family. But the scenario above depicts a generation-long discipleship process that needs to be repeated in homes everywhere. If an area of service—worship, working in clubs, mission trips, community service, Sunday school, or whatever appeals to you and yours—becomes a family activity, it will be a prime tool for the discipleship of your children.

Michelle and Michael Bowen from Missouri serve together in ministry. Michelle wrote me the following:

My husband [Michael] oversees our Wednesday night ministry and is the director for both VBS and overnight camps. I serve as his assistant. My mother-in-law helps us with the children under five in all these adventures, and [Michael's] brother and sister-in-law also serve (usually with the older children). I grew up in a family who went to church, but never had a personal relationship with God. They sat in a pew—they may even have put a check in the plate from time to time—but there was nothing outside of that. Living in this family is like night and day. Our children (ages 11 months to 6 years) go with us everywhere. They are there for the children's programming (even if they are too young), they are there for the planning meetings, and they come with me when I visit with mothers of the clubbers. What do I notice about my children? I notice that they have a heart for others. When they see a need that someone has, they ask if they can help, and before Michael or I can answer, they usually have a plan of how they want to help. When they see someone hurting, they offer to pray. My children aren't especially outgoing, yet they are sensitive to the needs of others, and they understand that serving God's people is serving God. To them, it's a way of life. I can't possibly think of a better form of discipleship than to bring my children with me when I serve!

How to Get Families to Be Involved Together

Let's get down to nuts and bolts. Now that you're convinced (I trust!) of the value of families ministering together, how do you go about implementing this principle in your own church or organization? Like any significant change in the way things are done, this will be a process, and there may be some bumps in the road as you go. The following steps will help you lead your workers (and potential workers) into this new way of thinking about and doing ministry.

> Youth and children's ministry are not places for parents to disciple their own children spiritually but rather a time for their children to observe them ministering.

Begin by Casting the Vision

If you talk regularly about the importance of family involvement in ministry, you will in time see some results. Remember that few people are early adapters, and most will need to hear the idea repeatedly before they begin to catch on.

Some parents who already serve in the ministry where their children are will need to have their vision adjusted. Which ones? The parents who are there primarily for their own kids. Help them to see that youth and children's ministry are not places for them to train their own kids spiritually (they can do that at home), but *rather a time for their children to observe them ministering.* This adjustment of vision will have a very positive effect on the child and on the ministry as well.

Evaluate Your Ministries

Before you start making changes, you'll want to take a good look at what you've already got. Here are some questions you may find helpful as you assess your current situation:

1. Does your church activity calendar allow for family participation? If, say, a dad in your church and his teenage daughter wanted to serve in a ministry that his six-year-old son participated in, could it happen? Debbie Broyles, a friend of mine from California, described a mom who made great use of this kind of opportunity:

   > I think of the Hanley family. The youngest, Josh, is now a senior in high school. The first four were girls, and as each one started high school, Mom discipled them to run a department in Vacation Bible School. I didn't think Josh would get involved, because he is a guy. But then I got a call, and Mom asked if 14-year-old Josh could run a department, and she would stay in the background and make sure everything ran well. Today, I have no doubt that he could run a Bible School no matter where he went as a young adult. [The experience of running a VBS department] has given the kids in this family confidence in their own spiritual ability, and they know what is involved no matter where they go or where they serve the Lord.

2. If you had a family that wanted to worship together in your church (meaning all the kids stayed in the worship service with their parents), could they do it? How would others perceive that?

3. If you had a family that wanted to learn (e.g., attend a Sunday school class or Bible study) together in your church, could they do it? How would that be perceived?

4. If you had a family that wanted to participate in fellowship together, could they do it? How would others perceive that?

5. What ministry opportunities are there where a 9-to-12-year-old could serve along with his or her parents?

6. Are all of your youth group service activities planned for youth-alone ministry, or are there opportunities for teenagers to serve in leadership with their parents or in programs with their younger siblings?

7. When you look at the grade-specific programs of your church, what patterns do you see in parental involvement?

8. What attitudes in children's and youth ministry workers do you detect about families serving or being together? What about in the parents themselves?

Create Opportunities

So many times, families aren't involved together simply because we don't create the opportunities. Here are a few types of ministry that can be conducive to family participation:

1. Evening VBS is something many churches are trying because it can fit into the schedules of family members of all ages.

2. Club ministries or sports outreach ministries usually have a variety of positions that can be filled by various members of a family.

3. Church-initiated neighborhood ministries, in which church families find a way to serve a neighbor, are something that more congregations are finding to be successful.

4. Family mission trips were unheard of 30 years ago, but are a very real possibility now. Want to make a significant impact on your kids? A trip to visit missionary friends, or a ministry you support, will deeply influence their worldview and create a life-long memory for your whole family.

Begin Recruiting Family Members of Existing Workers

You likely already have a group of people committed to assisting you with your ministry. Encouraging those volunteers to involve their family members in the work is a great place to start nurturing family ministry. Taking the following steps will help you handle this process smoothly:

1. Have a "Spouse Day" and invite the spouses of your workers to come and just see what goes on. Or make it a "Family Day" and invite older children to watch their parents serve.

2. Make a list of your workers whose spouses or other family members could potentially get involved with them.

3. Talk to the workers on your list and personally share your idea with them. You absolutely want your current volunteer's approval before you approach his or her family member(s).

4. Include your worker in the conversation when you talk
   to his or her family member(s).

What to Do When Parents Mess It Up

Some ministry leaders are reluctant to have parents work with
their kids' ministries. This is especially true in youth work, but
this reluctance also seeps down into children's ministry. Some
hesitate because of prior negative experiences; others resist because they fear what *might* be. None of us want a negative experience if we can avoid it.

Maybe you are concerned that parents working with their kids
might create problems. Your concern may well be valid, but don't
just set a policy that parents can never be involved in programs
where their own kids are present; find a better solution. Since most
of the problems come from parents not knowing how to treat their
own child equally with the others, there are things you can do to
address this specific issue. First, you'll need to identify what kind
of parent problem you have. Here are three kinds of parents you
may encounter when families are involved together:

1. *The "American Idol" Parent.* "American Idol" parents
   beam from ear to ear when their children answer questions correctly, make insightful comments, or in any
   other way stand out from the crowd. They encourage
   their children to occupy the spotlight, even if the children don't want to. They want others to see that their
   children are the spiritual ones—the stars. They're no
   different from the Little League dad who wants his little Hubert to become the next major leaguer, except
   that their arena for stardom is the church. They are
   likely not conscious of the fact that they give their own
   children preferential treatment. The children, however,
   are often aware of, and may take advantage of, their
   preferred positions. This can greatly disrupt a ministry.
   These issues can arise when "Idol" parents' children

are present as students, but may also occur when their children are assistant teachers or leaders.

2. *The "Mayberry" Parent.* Because they are in the room, "Mayberry" parents expect that their children will always be well behaved, and they are absolutely mortified when their little "Opie Taylors" mess up. Even when other volunteers are working with their children, they jump in to correct or discipline. They will often be harsher with their own children than with the others—partly in order to avoid their own embarrassment. Their harshness may make the other volunteers back off from them and can destroy teamwork. It can also be damaging to their children's self-worth, not to mention their desire to participate in ministry activities.

3. *The "Simpsons" Parent.* The opposite of the "Mayberry" parent, this mom or dad is oblivious to little "Bart's" antics. Disciplining their own children, or seeing their own children disciplined, is what embarrasses "Simpsons" parents. They're very content to let their kids run loose, and they get quite offended if other workers try to control them. Secretly (well, maybe not), the other workers are deeply frustrated with the children, but more so with the parents. This frustration can even lead to a worker saying, "If So-and-so is going to be working in this group next year, I'm not coming back."

In discipline cases involving the child of a parent volunteer, opinions about how the situation was handled tend to form very quickly. If the child's parent handles it, other parents can become critical if he or she doesn't handle it correctly in their eyes. If another volunteer does it, the parent of the child who is being corrected may be extra sensitive to how that kind of situation is handled.

So what do you do? Here are several things I've found to be helpful:

1. Talk about these issues *before* the families get involved together. Talk about them with both the parents and the children. Before they serve, help parents to identify what tendencies they have when working in a ministry with their own kids.

2. Help parents to see that during the ministry time, they are not a parent of their own child but a shepherd of all of the children. If there's something they feel they need to address as a parent, insist that they do it outside of the group time. Give them a vision for how important it is for their child to observe them ministering to others.

3. Place parents in the same ministry as their children, but probably not leading the small groups their children are in. If their ministry has a small group segment, assign them to other kids.

4. Have a clear discipline procedure and structure in place. In particular, address *before* a problem occurs how you will handle a discipline situation that involves one of your volunteers' children. Here are some suggestions:

   • Every child is to be treated with respect, grace and love.
   • The director of the program is the only one to handle individual discipline issues. When a child of a parent who is present is disruptive and rebellious, the adult worker takes that child to the director, whether that child is his/hers or not.
   • Workers other than the director (including parents of children in the program) may handle group inattention and disorder.
   • Parents do not interfere when their children are in another group and are disruptive; everyone respects the chain of command.

- A volunteer worker is responsible for the order and respect of the children assigned to him or her, even if a child in the group has a parent in the room.
- The director of the program will handle all concerns regarding the treatment of the child.

I strongly encourage you to involve families together. Doing so will strengthen your ministry, improve your workers' faithfulness, and further disciple the kids. How can it get better than that?

Think and Talk About It

1. Imagine you are a worker on the wall in Jerusalem. Why would it have been encouraging for you to hear that Nehemiah was arranging workers according to their families?

2. Think about your workers. What are your observations about whether or not they serve together with other family members?

3. Can you cite an instance when family members serving together had a positive impact on either the family or the ministry (or both)?

4. Can you think of a time when family members serving together was a problem? How was the problem handled?

5. If the problem from Question 4 resulted in family members no longer serving together, how could the situation have been dealt with so that family involvement could have been preserved?

6. Who in your church or organization needs to be persuaded of the "families involved together" approach? How might you start to do that?

7. Look again through the section "How to Get Families to Be Involved Together." What do you think you might be able to start to do within the next couple of weeks to bring family involvement in ministry to your church or organization?

FOCUS, PEOPLE, FOCUS

After I looked things over, I stood up and said to the nobles,
the officials and the rest of the people, "Don't be afraid of them.
Remember the Lord, who is great and awesome, and fight."
NEHEMIAH 4:14

Uzziel here again.

I have to tell you, I was in for some surprises when I got together with my family. I was so excited to see them and to work together with them on the wall! But I didn't expect what I heard from them. My dad, Harhaiah, wasn't feeling well at all. I think I told you already that his health isn't the best, and it was showing. But what really surprised me was the conversation I had with my brothers, Azariah and Pediah. Even though the city of Jerusalem isn't all that big, we had been so busy we hadn't had an opportunity to talk since work on the wall began. They had been working on the east side, closer to some of the main roads, so they had heard more of the talk from other workers on the wall. Azariah started the conversation:

"Uzziel, it's great to see you. We weren't sure where you were working, or how you were doing. No offense, but if you feel as bad as you look, you've been working way too hard," Azariah chuckled.

"No question about that," I answered. "Just look at my hands. They're just raw. No good for any goldsmithing for a while."

Pediah joined the conversation: "Hey, Uzziel, I see you're back. It's good to have you here. Look, I know you've been working really hard, but Azariah and I have been talking, and we think this wall is a lost cause. I'd hate to think that what you have done to your hands was for nothing, but everyone we talk to is so exhausted they're ready to quit. We just don't see how it is going to get done."

"Yeah," Azariah added, "and is it really that important? After all, we lived with the wall the way it was for a lot of years. True, it was a little embarrassing, but …"

"But what if the Arabs attack, like they're planning?" Pediah finished Azariah's thought. "They will probably just tear it down again, and we'd be right back where we started."

"And look at Dad," Azariah lowered his voice. "He can't do any more. At least, he shouldn't. He wants to, though, and if this goes forward, he's going to kill himself or at least get pretty sick because he's trying too hard."

I could see they were ready to quit. And to be honest, what they were saying made me think. Like Pediah, I wasn't sure we would be able to finish the wall.

The sound of horses approaching interrupted my thoughts. We looked out into the road, and to my amazement, it was Nehemiah and his men again. "How are you doing, men?" Nehemiah started the conversation.

"Great," Azariah lied. "Thanks for putting us together as families."

Pediah wasn't about to paint such a rosy picture. "Uzziel here is not in very good shape. Just look at his hands." I tried to stop him from saying anything—I didn't want Nehemiah to know how I was feeling—but I was too late. Pediah went on, "Our father, Harhaiah, is inside—in pain because he's been working so hard. Did you know a lot of people are talking about quitting?"

I was surprised by Nehemiah's face. He didn't flinch, and he didn't frown—in fact, he didn't react negatively at all. He said, "I've been looking things over, and I would like you to come to a gathering of the workers over by the East Gate. We're meeting right away." And with that, he rode off to tell others.

Pediah, Azariah and I looked at each other. "Okay, let's get Dad and go."

When we got to the East Gate, the nobles and other bigwigs were there, as well as many of the workers. Nehemiah arrived shortly after we did, and he immediately stood up in front of the people. One look at his face, and you could tell that his whole being was behind what he was about to say. Everything about him told us his message would be highly important and extremely significant. His chin began quivering, as if he were fighting back emotion. He looked over the whole crowd, and it seemed like he was trying to connect gazes with everyone that was there. The whole crowd grew quiet. He waited until there was no sound at all besides a slight rustling of the wind.

Then he began. He spoke quietly at first, pausing after every word to let it sink in: "Don't be afraid of them." Then he raised both fists in the air, took a huge breath, and looked at everyone again. Then, with what I think was the loudest shout I have ever heard, he gave us his battle cry: "Remember the Lord, who is great and awesome." It was so full of emotion, so full of heart, and such a startling cry that, for a few seconds, no one moved or reacted. Then, Pediah—my brother, of all people—broke the silence. We were standing near the back, and with emotion and volume nearly matching Nehemiah's, he shouted in response, "Remember the Lord." It was so sudden and so unexpected that, for a moment, everyone turned and just looked. Then a man near the front—Shallum, I think it was—echoed Pediah's call. Then another shouted, then four or five together, and then suddenly more and more until the whole group turned to face Nehemiah with a unison echo of his words. It was awesome, awesome, awesome. I don't think the chanting died down for at least eight to ten minutes. When everyone was worn out from the shouting, the silence returned, and everyone waited for Nehemiah to continue. His eyes had misted. It was clear he knew we had caught his message. Then, quiet as at first, he said, "Men, you have to fight. You have to fight for your brothers." He paused and looked into our eyes again. "You must fight for your sons. You must fight for your daughters." Another pause. "You must fight for your wives. You must fight for your houses." And with that, he got back on his horse and rode away.

No one moved for a while. No one even talked. Suddenly I realized that he hadn't said anything about how tired we were feeling. It occurred to me that he didn't talk about how much work there was still to do, or even say how much we had completed. "Remember the Lord" was really his whole message to us. The words kept coming back. I could hear his determination when he said them, and the response of everyone shouting those words back to him still stirred me inside.

I marveled. Then, his words began to remind me of the first time I met him. At that time, he had told us of the miraculous things God had done to bring him to Jerusalem. He had made it clear that God would be the one to give us success. Nehemiah was just being consistent by telling us, "Remember the Lord." Gradually I began to get it. Yes, the Lord would be the one to give us strength. He alone could defeat our enemies. He could help us finish the wall. "Nehemiah's right," I told Pediah and Azariah. "Just remember the Lord. Let's get back to work and get this wall done!"

The Number One Job of a Leader

Keeping people focused on the right thing in ministry is the *job* of a leader; in fact, it is the *number one* job. To some of us, it comes more naturally; others of us have to work on it. But no matter how God has wired us, if He has placed us in ministry, it is our responsibility to help our workers stay on track.

On the other hand, Satan is all about misdirection. Just like in Nehemiah's day, he will distract us through enemies, or through our physical condition, or through rumors or gossip—the list is endless. The effective ministry leader is always on the alert for those distractions and will counteract them with a clear call to focus. That is exactly what Nehemiah did.

> Keeping people focused on the right thing is the number one job of a leader.

For the ministry leader today, the million-dollar question is, "What *is* the right focus?" To answer that question, let's start by thinking through what makes you tick.

What makes you pound the podium?

You may not literally be a podium-pounder, but I'm sure you know what I mean: There is something that you are deeply passionate about. It is something that so stirs you that if you're up in front of your volunteers speaking about it, you *might* pound the podium to make your point. This is the thing that kindles your emotion—that makes your heart burn within you. It is what *really* lights your fire.

In your ministry, what is it for you? Before you answer that question, let's look at what it was for Nehemiah.

Nehemiah's Focus

Consider this question: What did Nehemiah go to Jerusalem to do? Ask people that, and most who have heard the story will answer, "To rebuild the wall there." But that's wrong. That's not why he went.

In Nehemiah 1, we read of the report Hanani gave to him about Jerusalem, and his response: "'Those who survived the exile and are back in the province are in great trouble and disgrace. The wall of Jerusalem is broken down, and its gates have been burned with fire.' When I heard these things, I sat down and wept. For some days I mourned and fasted and prayed before the God of heaven" (Neh. 1:3-4).

I struggled for a time to understand. "Why would Nehemiah mourn and fast and pray for days over a broken-down wall?" I wondered. In chapter 2, he is so concerned over the situation in Jerusalem that his face can't hide his feelings. As I studied, it just didn't make sense to me that stones strewn over the ground should produce so much dejection. Then I paid closer attention to Nehemiah 2:17: "Then I said to them, 'You see the trouble we are in: Jerusalem lies in ruins, and its gates have been burned with fire. Come, let us rebuild the wall of Jerusalem, and we will no longer be in disgrace.'"

> Nehemiah was driven by the disgrace, not by the broken-down wall.

Finally, I understood: The *spiritual disgrace* was the reason Nehemiah felt such a burden; rebuilding the wall was the practical way the disgrace would be removed. While Nehemiah would not have mourned and fasted for days over piles of stones, he did have that response to the reputation of God being tarnished. He was driven by the disgrace, not by the broken-down wall. Do you see?

Mourning and fasting were the ways Nehemiah responded to his *heart* being stirred. This was how he "pounded the podium."

As I continued in the text, armed with my newfound understanding of Nehemiah's core purpose, I heard Nehemiah's chapter 4 exhortation to the people to "Remember the Lord!" as a war cry of sorts. There have been other similar ones in our history: "Remember the Alamo" in the Texas Revolution, "Remember the Maine" in the Spanish-American War, "Remember the Lusitania" in World War I, and "Remember Pearl Harbor" in World War II. In each case, the call was to remember a grievous injustice and offense against the American people. Nehemiah must have felt just as strongly (if not more strongly) about the disgrace brought on the reputation of God through the broken-down wall.

The Right Focus

Still, I'm sure there was a temptation for everyone involved, including Nehemiah, to become more concerned about building the wall than removing the disgrace. We face similar temptations in ministry today. Know what I mean? Of course, in the ministry God has called us to, the distractions have different names, but the tension is the same:

Not the wall ...	But the disgrace ...
Not the organization ...	But the ministry ...
Not the program ...	But the discipleship ...
Not the delivery of the lesson ...	But the truth learned ...
Not the schedule ...	But the heart touched ...
Not the latest technology ...	But the life changed ...

This distinction is critical for you in ministry. If *you* have the wrong focus in your heart, it will be virtually impossible for you to develop the right focus in your people.

As a ministry leader, I'm sure your life is filled with event after event. Whether it's Sunday morning ministry or something else, here's a question for you: When your ministry event is over, and you say (to yourself, if not to someone else), "That really went well!" what made you say that?

The organization? "Yes! Everything went just like clockwork."

The presentation? "Yes! The whole team pulled it off perfectly."

The technology? "That video turned out absolutely flawlessly!"

Or was it discipleship? Truth learned? Hearts touched? And lives changed?

Organization, presentations, schedules, and the effective use of technology and other tools are means that will help you accomplish the true ends of ministry, but they must not be your passion—your heart's focus. They can't be what makes you pound the podium.

I've seen it done the wrong way, and I've done it the wrong way myself; I'm sure you have, too. I used to run large events for children in the Los Angeles area as part of my ministry with Awana. Twice we rented UCLA's large basketball arena, Pauley Pavilion, and held our inter-club competition there. The purpose was twofold: (1) to connect with parents who might not otherwise ever attend church and present the gospel to them, and (2) to motivate the children to learn God's truth (they had to memorize a certain amount of Scripture to attend). Each time, the event was incredible! More than 4,000 children participated, 6,000-plus parents and grandparents were in attendance, more than 1,000 volunteers helped pull it off, and everything went like clockwork. In looking back, though, I have to confess that in my heart, I was more focused on the organization and pageantry of the event than I was on the spiritual purposes. In fact, I was so distracted that it took a ministry volunteer to alert me to my misplaced focus.

It happened at a planning meeting. We were well into the organizational process, discussing recruitment of staff, schedule and procedures, when Jeanne, one of the volunteers, asked, "So, what are we doing as far as the spiritual emphasis?" I fumbled for an answer because I hadn't thought that far yet. I'd thought about all the other things, but not about the most important one. Her words, though she intended them only as a question, were a quiet rebuke to me, because I knew I had neglected the core issue. When the day came and went, we did see God do some great things in parents' hearts, but I believe the event's impact might have been even greater if I had focused on the right thing sooner.

Having the right purpose starts with how you see the ministry that you lead. What is your heart's perception of what you are doing? I don't mean what your vision statement is; anyone can craft one of those. I'm talking about what drives you internally. Let's see how Nehemiah's passion worked itself out in the biblical account.

Nehemiah Refocuses the Workers

The workers were exhausted and discouraged. All they were seeing was the rubble, not the half-completed wall. They were focusing on their own weakness. How would Nehemiah refocus them? There were several possible strategies he could have employed:

He Could Have Focused on the Enemy

This kind of focus is the locker-room pep talk of a coach. Sometimes it's exactly what we need. If Nehemiah had done this, it might have sounded something like this:

> Are we going to let the Arabs and Ammonites win? Come on, people—if they can keep us from doing this, we will be under their thumbs forever! We're on God's side. They can't defeat us. Let's win here once and for all!

He Could Have Focused on the Work

This kind of focus acknowledges what has already been accomplished and affirms the workers' potential to do even more. It is encouraging and often appropriate. Nehemiah could have said:

> Look how much you've gotten done—you're halfway there! It may look like there are still a lot of stones, but look at the wall. Just *look* at it! You've made great progress here! All you need to do is keep it up, and we'll finish before you know it!

He Could Have Focused on Their Commitment

This kind of focus holds people accountable for the promise they made. Nehemiah could simply have said:

> People, you told me you would do this. Now, keep your word. Did you expect that this would be easy? Don't you be quitters! You committed to this, now stick with it!

He Could Have Focused on the Spiritual Purpose

This kind of focus keeps people from looking merely at the mechanics of ministry, and helps them keep the purpose in mind. Nehemiah could have reminded the people of the pressing concern that inspired them to join the work in the first place:

> Remember, people of Judah, we don't want the city of Jerusalem to be a blemish on the reputation of our God. Let's remove that disgrace!

I must say, I'm a little surprised that this wasn't the content of Nehemiah's pep talk to the people. But Nehemiah didn't do that.

He Turned Their Attention Back to God

> After I looked things over, I stood up and said to the nobles, the officials and the rest of the people, "Don't be afraid of them. Remember the Lord, who is great and awesome, and fight" (Neh. 4:14).

The very best focus is a God-focus. A. W. Tozer, one of the most-quoted pastors of the twentieth century, once said, "What comes into our minds when we think about God is the most important thing about us." Therefore, if we can get our workers to rightly focus on God—His person and His character—all other motivations and actions will flow properly from that thinking.

So, Nehemiah picked the most excellent approach. However, the other possibilities are not wrong—in fact, they are very appropriate at times. For example, the apostle Paul encouraged Timothy to focus on the *activity* of ministry when he told him, "Preach the Word" (2 Tim. 4:2). Yet in the story of Nehemiah, when the workers struggled to maintain their focus and commitment, their leader knew the best thing for him to do was to point them straight back to God.

More often than not, that's going to be the wisest thing for you to do, too.

How to Get Your Workers to Focus

How do you help your workers focus on the right thing? I want to share three principles that I have learned through my experience:

1. Be a shepherd, not a cowboy.
2. Select a single, simple focus—until they get it.
3. Review, repeat and remind.

Be a Shepherd, Not a Cowboy

I know personally why the Bible never calls Jesus "the Good Cowboy" or commands ministry leaders to "cowboy your herd."

I grew up on a cattle ranch in western Nebraska. My father and grandfather had a medium-sized ranch, which was divided into about eight different "pastures." The ranch was in the Sandhills, a region of treeless, gently rolling hills covered with natural grass. Our cattle were separated into different herds, and a regular part of ranch life was moving them from pasture to pasture. We did this partly to keep the grass from being eaten down too much, which would stunt its growth, and partly to keep the cattle where the eating was the best.

When we moved the cattle from one pasture to another, we called it a "cattle drive." I'm sure you've never heard of a "sheep drive," right? There's a reason: You don't *drive* sheep.

We'd get the horses and our old pickup truck, and first we would round up the cattle. They would be scattered throughout the pasture, so we would start driving them toward the center of the pasture they were in. We would yell at them ("heee-aaaah!"), honk the old pickup's horn, and even sometimes bump them with the horse to get them to start moving. Our dog, Ring, was a master at helping us, and he loved to get involved, too. He'd bark at the cattle and nip at their heels. We even had a bullwhip that we used—not to hit them, but more to "crack." The sound would certainly get their attention and motivate them to move.

Once we got them all together somewhere near the center of the pasture, the next thing to do was to get them through the gate and into the new pasture. We would work them from the back of the herd, getting some to move and heading off those who started going in the wrong direction. Eventually, they would all get the idea, and our little cattle drive from one pasture to another would be successful.

This kind of technique works with cattle, but it would throw chaos and panic into a flock of sheep. Think about the differences:

With cattle, you . . .	With sheep, you . . .
Drive them from behind	Lead them from in front
Yell, honk the horn, and crack the whip	*Call them*
Focus first on those farthest away	Focus first on the closest ones
Send the dog out to get them all moving	*Use the dog to control the strays*

As a side note, one thing that works with both cattle and sheep is food. If they're hungry, both will follow you if they think you've got food for them. Volunteers aren't so different, are they?

In order to best help your workers focus on the right thing, you must use the right approach—the approach of a shepherd, not a cowboy.

So what is the shepherd approach?

- First, you call to them. That means that you are already heading in the direction that you want them to go, and you're inviting them to come with you.
- Then, you must *lead* them, not drive them. Just as with sheep, trying to drive volunteers results in chaos (and resignations).
- Finally, you get a few to follow. Once a few are following, others will pay attention; gradually, more will fall into step until your "flock" is going in the direction you want.

Nehemiah's words are the words of a shepherd, not a cowboy. He isn't chiding his workers or attempting to make them feel guilty; his words give them direction.

What's *your* natural tendency? When you want your people to focus, are you more of a cowboy? If you are, keep that tendency in check and learn to *call* your workers to new efforts or a new direction. Then lead them there—just like a shepherd.

Select a Single, Simple Focus—Until They Get It

It's interesting to me that Nehemiah's message to encourage the workers is so brief. In fact, he only needs eight words to make his point: "Don't be afraid. Remember the Lord, and fight!" We don't know if he spoke for two hours, and this is just his summary, or if his address to the wall workers was really this brief. But if it was a longer speech, it was certainly summarized easily.

One Focus at a Time

What focus do you choose for your workers? I have asked children's and youth ministry leaders to finish this sentence: "I wish my workers would . . ." Listed below are 25 sample responses. Read through the list and see how many you identify with.

1. Be on time
2. Be more committed
3. See the big picture
4. Tell me when they're not going to be there
5. Be more community-minded
6. Love each other
7. Come to planning meetings
8. See how important ministering to children is
9. Pray together more
10. Be mentored their first year by an experienced youth worker
11. Have all the tools and resources they need
12. Be more consistent in their attendance
13. Take more of a leadership role
14. Love the Lord with all their heart, soul and mind
15. Really comprehend the impact they're having on kids' lives
16. Pray for their students
17. Take the initiative
18. Use the lessons I give them
19. Follow guidelines
20. Enjoy the ministry—have fun!
21. Step out in faith more often and do what they've not done before

22. Love all the children equally
23. Contribute well-thought-out ideas and suggestions
24. Serve with passion as "unto the Lord"
25. Actually do what they say they are going to do

Of course, the list could have been a lot longer, but it's pretty representative of what is on the hearts of ministry leaders. As I heard each one, I found myself saying, "Oooh, yes!" "Yep—I identify with that!" "That person must know my workers!" Did you have similar thoughts? The list of things we *could* have our people focus on is loooooong . . . but to be effective, we must choose the best—and the most strategic—at any given time.

State It Simply

How do you help your people to *stay* focused? You want the objective to be easily remembered (if your instructions were so complicated that your workers can't recall what you said, there's little chance of them actually doing it), so that means that a short phrase or even a single word is best. Since the first time I studied this story of Nehemiah, the words "Remember the Lord" have stuck with me. It was easy. *Simple.* Just three words. But at the same time, so wise and profound.

Make It BASED

It was on the back of a dirty Ukrainian bus—about three o'clock in the morning—that BASED came to me. I was on my way to the Kiev airport, returning from a ministry trip. Even though I had only slept for a couple of hours before we started toward the airport, trying to get some rest was useless. The rough road and the lack of springs on the bus kept me wide awake, so I turned my thoughts to my ministry responsibilities.

My role as the director of training for Awana required that I clearly communicate our approach to what we produce and share with others. I had wanted, for a long time, to be able to simply but comprehensively describe what practical application of Scripture meant to me. I was frustrated with the definitions I was given in seminary, and had been searching for a unique way to express my training philosophy. And there in the back of that old bus, as my head rattled with the vibrations of the road and the bumps from potholes and rocks, I thought of BASED. I was thinking about 2 Timothy 3:16-17 when the clear progression of the words in those verses hit me—and then the acrostic BASE. Later, I added the concept of 2 Timothy 2:2 to complete it with a D.

Since that time, it has become the guiding formula for what I do and share in ministry. In fact, you should be able to see that this book contains all the elements except the D. Here is what BASED means:

The letter	Stands for	Answers this question	2 Timothy reference
B	Bible	What does the Bible say?	For doctrine (3:16)
A	Application	What should I do?	For reproof, for correction (3:16)
S	Specifics	How should I do it?	For instruction in righteousness (3:16)
E	Equipping	What do I need to do it?	Thoroughly equipped (3:17)
D	Discipleship	Will you show me how?	Commit to faithful men (2:2)

This simple acrostic has become the guiding formula for all our training in Awana—right down to our financial policy manual! It has become useful in several ways:

· It helps us to be *biblical*. It's crazy, but there's always the temptation in ministry to leave biblical truth out of the planning and strategy process. It's amazing how we want to teach the Bible, but we forget the Bible when we plan! The acrostic also reminds me to start with the Bible as well; in other words, *B* comes first.

- It helps us to be *balanced.* Lots of training—or strategy, or preaching, for that matter—is bAs (we tell them what they are to do, but give them little Bible, little specifics, and no tools or discipleship). Sometimes it's aSe—almost all specifics, with no biblical truth as the foundation. Sometimes, it is bAsEd. It's got all the elements, but the emphasis is on telling people what to do and giving them the tools. Most training is simply AS. But we strive to keep it balanced—we always want to be BASED.
- It helps us to *finish.* It is so easy to leave out the E, and even more so the D. It is pretty simple to tell people what to do and how they should do it, but providing the tools (E) is much harder. That takes more resources, and sometimes we don't have them. Harder still is to follow up with the D. This takes our most precious commodity—time. There are also some situations—like with me and you and this book— where the discipleship part is not possible to complete.

Apply BASED to a Focus

Select one thing you want your workers to focus on. If you like, you can write it on this line: _____
(the line is short, so you will be, too). Now evaluate your chosen goal. Is it a B, an A, an S, or an E? Here are some examples from our earlier list. I wish my workers would . . .

> Be more committed (this is an A)
> Come to planning meetings (S)
> Love the Lord with all their heart, soul and mind (B)
> Use the lessons I give them (E)

Finally, flesh it out. Is your phrase an A? Then find the biblical basis for your desire. Describe specifically how the goal will be accomplished. Think through what tools your workers will need to do it, and then how they will be discipled in the process. Here's an example:

> I would like my workers to focus on . . . praying for their kids.

That's an A, so now you have to think through B, S, E and D and how you will communicate each of those to your workers. The following chart is an example of a communication plan I would use if I were the ministry leader:

B	Colossians 1:9 (Paul praying for his disciples): "For this reason, since the day we heard about you, we have not stopped praying for you and asking God to fill you."
A	YOU pray for your kids (remember, they're YOUR disciples).
S	1. At 8:55, do a "5 for 5"—five volunteers get together for five minutes to pray for the kids in your ministry that morning. 2. At the beginning of each small group, start by praying for each of the kids in your group. 3. Keep a prayer list of your kids on your refrigerator, mirror, etc., so you are reminded to pray for them daily.
E	1. You'll get a text reminder at 8:25 about the prayer time. 2. In your packet is a schedule for you to follow in your small group; you will notice that prayer for your kids is listed first. 3. Here is a prayer card, with the names of those in your small group already listed on it. You'll need to add newcomers.
D	1. I will be in a "5 for 5" group myself every time. 2. I am going to demonstrate what I want you to do in your small group. Then, during our small-group time, I will be going from table to table to see how it is going for you. 3. I will be asking you if you are remembering to pray for your kids at home, and I will be bringing my list to show you how I am doing it.

Review, Repeat and Remind

The text of Nehemiah doesn't reveal whether or not he does this; we only read of his words being spoken once. Maybe the power of God was so present in his words to the workers that they stuck after being stated just once. I'm sure you agree with me that it is very rare today for our workers to retain what we said after we've just said it once. We all know we need to review, remind and repeat things in order for people to remember.

How do you do this? You may be familiar with a passage in Deuteronomy about teaching children: "These commandments

> Your focus must permeate your own communication—especially your verbal communication.

that I give you today are to be upon your hearts. Impress them on your children. Talk about them when you sit at home and when you walk along the road, when you lie down and when you get up. Tie them as symbols on your hands and bind them on your foreheads. Write them on the doorframes of your houses and on your gates" (Deut. 6:6-9).

These verses of Scripture give us a pattern:

1. *Alter your vocabulary.* The first specific command of Deuteronomy 6 concerning impressing God's words upon children is "talk." Talk when you sit, talk when you walk, talk when you lie down, and talk when you get up. In other words, saturate your daily conversations with talk about God. In leading workers, follow the same principle: Your focus must permeate your own communication—especially your verbal communication. What do you want your workers to focus on? Whatever it is, say it when you teach them, when you pray, and when you are in informal conversations. Talk it!

2. *Create constant reminders.* Deuteronomy 6:8 describes putting God's words where you will be constantly reminded of them: on the backs of your hands (what you see) and on your forehead (what others see). Follow the same principle with your focus. Today it's not the backs of hands or the middle of foreheads (well, it might be), but it is newsletters, texts, emails, etc. Keep your focus constantly before your people (and yourself).

3. *Decorate your environment.* Deuteronomy 6:9 describes putting God's words in the prominent spots in your environment: your doorframes (the last thing you see

before you leave your house) and your gates (the first thing other people see when entering). Let me encourage you to follow the same principle with your focus. I love visiting children's ministry areas in churches; they are usually decorated with so much color and creativity. And then there's the youth area . . . always made to look "cool." I think there are three ways to decorate a children's ministry room, and I believe it is possible, and beneficial, to accomplish all three in one room.

- Decorate to attract the student. You've heard about it if you haven't seen it, and you've probably salivated over it if you don't have it: the décor fit to rival Disneyland. That is what I'm talking about here.

- Decorate to educate the student. This usually means biblical scenes portrayed, and maybe biblical truths written out.

- Decorate to inform and guide the teacher. Usually, this is done around the upper part of the room where students' eyes don't go as much. This serves as a cross-curriculum and cross-ministry guide to teachers using the room so that there is consistency.

When you talk about your focus, create reminders and decorate accordingly, you will effectively keep that focus before your workers and help them to move steadily toward it.

Think and Talk About It

1. Think through the circumstances surrounding Nehemiah's words, "Remember the Lord." Why do you think these words were so appropriate in that context?

2. Scan again the section on pages 75-76 titled "The Right Focus." Make a list from your ministry situation of right and wrong focuses.

3. Is your natural tendency to be more of a shepherd or a cowboy?

4. What do you think would be the best focus for your ministry workers right now?

5. Work through the BASED approach to flesh out your chosen focus. See if you can describe all the elements.

6. How do you plan to repeat your focus and remind your workers of it, and for how long?

PERSONAL MEANING

*"Fight for your brothers, your sons and your daughters,
your wives and your homes."*
NEHEMIAH 4:14

"Daddy make wall?"

My little Malkijah, who was born two summers ago, had taken my sore, bruised hand in his little ones and was looking intently at my palm. It was about noontime. I had finished a long morning of placing stones about 50 yards south of our house, and had just returned home for a short rest and a drink. As usual, he came toddling out to meet me as soon as he saw me. I looked forward to that so much each time I went back to my house. The other boys were a little older, and were often involved in their play, but Malkijah was always watching for me to come home. As he looked at my hand, I thought, *Malkijah is without a doubt the handsome one. His deep brown eyes look so much like his mother's!* I suspect he is going to have my height, and probably my eye for detail. I think he will be the one who will love working with gold like his dad—maybe the one to take over the family business some day.

I noticed his hair, too: his too-long curls hid some dirt around his ears. "All boy," I commented to myself. I've reflected many times since coming back home how hard it was to be away from him and his two brothers—and how thankful I am to be able to work on the wall near my house and family.

His comment, though, amazed me. He had said, "Daddy make wall?" after looking at my hand. He made the connection between the condition of my hand and the work I had been doing. He was pretty young for that! Pretty observant for a two-year-old, if I do say so myself!

"Yes, son, Daddy has been making the wall," I answered. But I wasn't prepared for what Malkijah did next. He pushed me to sit down so he could climb up on my lap, and then he put his little arms around my neck and tucked his head between my shoulder and my beard. He turned his face toward mine, toward my ear, and said quietly, "T'ank you, Daddy." I moved his head so I could talk in his ear. "For what, son?" I whispered. I wasn't really sure what he was referring to.

His face showed a hint of frustration because I didn't get what he was saying. "For you make wall." I never thought that he could understand that the wall was to protect him, but—somehow—he must be getting it.

It made me remember Nehemiah's words when he spoke to us: "Fight for your sons," he had said. I thought about protecting Malkijah from the enemies ... about providing a safe place for him to play ... about making a good home for my whole family ... and I knew—I *had* to get this wall built by my house.

"Daddy's got to get back to work," I said to my boy as I lifted him off my lap.

Finding Personal Meaning

Nehemiah had told the people, "Fight for your brothers, your sons and your daughters, your wives and your homes." Do you understand the significance of what he said? Brothers . . . sons . . . daughters . . . wives . . . homes . . . What is more meaningful to a man in this life than the people and things on that list? Nehemiah made the fight *personal*. His words reminded his workers, "This is not merely for some cause—this fight is for you—and for the things most dear to you."

I live in a suburb of Chicago. As I am writing this manuscript, the news has been full of reports about the rash of earthquakes—first in Haiti, then in Chile, northern Mexico and, more recently, China. I was riveted by the news about Haiti, where I personally know one family. I was so relieved when word came that they were okay. I don't know anyone in Chile or China, so while I was shocked by the reports from those places, they didn't have the same emotional effect on me.

But do you know what I was thinking about most as the earthquake stories dominated the news?

Ryan and Kirsti [my son and daughter-in-law] live in southern California . . .

Southern California is on a big earthquake fault, too . . .

It's been a while since there's been an earthquake there.

Isn't it interesting that the news of tragedy in other parts of the world caused my thoughts to go toward southern California? Why did my thoughts fly in that direction? Because part of my *family* is there. I have been concerned about Chile and China, but that is nothing compared to what I would feel if the news were about a major earthquake in southern California.

> You must do everything you can to help your workers find *personal* meaning in the ministry they are involved in.

Nehemiah understood this principle, and with his words, he gave the work personal meaning.

That's your job as a leader of people: You must do everything you can to help them find *personal meaning* in the ministry they are involved in.

"Larry, will you pray for our ministry?" I got that call about 10:30 on a Wednesday night. It came from Shelly, who oversaw the Awana club ministry in a church that I worked with. I knew this church's story. It had nearly died, and a new pastor, who felt it was his life's calling to rescue dying churches, had come about a year before. This pastor felt strongly that a children's outreach was an important key to rebuilding a church, so he had started Awana in the church. God was blessing, and this little church, which had been so tired and discouraged, was bursting with life once again.

But Shelly's voice was full of concern. "I had two leaders separately come to me tonight and tell me they needed to quit. They said that their work schedules were getting really full, and they just couldn't do everything anymore."

Shelly explained further, "The hard part is, they are both men. In fact, they are the only two men we've got in our ministry, and there aren't many more in our church who are prospects to take their place. Will you pray with me? I don't know what I'm going to do."

I promised I would pray. I did, but I'm sure Shelly prayed a lot more. I didn't hear from her for two weeks. Then—late Wednesday evening again—she called. Her voice was entirely different. "You remember how I asked you to pray for my two male leaders?" I could hear the excitement.

"Yes . . ." I replied.

"God answered prayer!" Shelly was *pumped*. "God answered prayer in a special way tonight."

"What happened?" She had my complete attention.

"Tonight Pastor John spoke to the children and presented the gospel to them. It was great—the kids listened intently, and I believe God was really working in their hearts. At the end, he told the kids that if they wanted to understand the gospel better and respond, they should go to their favorite leader, and he or she would help them.

"Well, we had two boys respond tonight! They did exactly what Pastor John asked them to—they went to their favorite leaders. And guess who they went to talk to—the two men that I told you were going to quit. Each of those men had the privilege of leading a child to Jesus tonight!

"As I talked with them afterward, they each told me something else—they said, 'If *this* is what we get to do, *we're not going to quit after all!'*"

What was the difference? What changed the minds of these two men? They got to personally experience the greatest blessing of ministry—seeing someone new being born into God's family. No doubt they had been *giving out*, but that night they experienced the joy of *receiving*, and they received through participating in the harvest.

Yes, the two boys received Christ. That was the most important victory. But there was another: The two men found personal meaning in ministry.

Shelly never expected that God would answer the way He did. But in addition to meeting her ministry need, God also reminded me of a critical principle through that incident: People are less likely to quit if they find personal satisfaction and meaning in their ministry.

> People are less likely to quit if they find personal satisfaction and meaning in their ministry.

What Gives Personal Meaning to Ministry?

Knowing it's important for people to find personal meaning in their ministry isn't enough. If we're going to help our volunteers reach that level of involvement, we need to understand what kinds of things provide meaning and fulfillment to workers. I asked several of my ministry friends this question, and here is a sample of what they told me:

> I grow closer to the Lord. As the children ask questions, it drives me deeper into the Word to be sure I am giving accurate answers. Working with children also helps me have the faith of a little child. (Bill Gunter, Pennsylvania)

I have grown spiritually in more ways than I can imagine! Most importantly, children have taught me that faith is all about "keeping it real." (Pam Hanson, Nebraska)

The Christian faith is not complicated. As adults, we make it complicated. We "deep think" things and make it complicated. Children are simple folks. They believe what it is and do what it says. They are an encouragement to me to walk my faith simply and unconditionally. (Dan Novak, Missouri)

I'm more likely to study God's Word in preparation for lessons. I spend more time in prayer. I'm more likely to bring it home and spend more time with my own kids teaching them. I'm more careful of things I say and do because kids tend to pick up on the smallest things . . . therefore, it's become a natural part of my daily life to just live more for Christ. (Mel Jones, Nebraska)

I recently received a note from one of "my kids" who found me via Facebook. She thanked me for the role I had played in her life and then said she was one of my "spiritual children" and shared that she had come to know and love Jesus through our Kids Church program. Being reminded of the eyes that watch—even decades later—is *great* accountability. (Jane Ann Larson, Iowa)

I have grown in the knowledge and love of God's Word; I have grown in compassion. Working with kids sparks my creativity and desire to serve, so I get to use my gifts and talents for the Kingdom. (Pauline Limberg, Illinois)

Trevor loves me. That has changed me. This little guy came in speaking like a sailor, openly challenging every adult. He was tough and tougher to handle. Trevor is teaching me how to love—something I thought I had learned. (Tom Rios, California)

The Sweet Spot

The first way you, as a leader, can help your workers find more personal meaning in ministry is by making sure each of them is in his or her sweet spot.

What is a "sweet spot"? In baseball, it's the part of the bat most likely to send the ball flying a good long way when contact is made. There's science involved, but what's important to fans of the game is this: Hit the ball with the sweet spot of your bat, and it's a thing of beauty. Volunteers have sweet spots, too—those places in ministry where they are best able to connect and make a positive impact.

If you've been a ministry leader for a while, you've probably got a story that goes something like this: You had someone volunteer, and while his or her heart was good, the ministry position was not a good fit. It resulted in muck all around.

Randy is such a person. He was a co-worker of mine—deeply devoted to God and exemplary in his personal walk. Excited about working with kids, he volunteered for a ministry leadership position that involved attention to detail. Randy was and is a great guy—no, an incredible guy—but attention to detail is like a foreign language to him. He would forget supplies, miscount, and fail to communicate things like starting times. Everything Randy touched as an administrator turned into a mess. He upset people, frustrated plans, and I'm sure felt very frustrated himself. The truth that his leadership was a failure was painful for him and for his ministry supervisor who had to move him. But Randy's failure in one area of ministry didn't mean he couldn't serve God well—he just had to find his sweet spot. Today, he has a teaching/preaching role in ministry and is thriving. He is discipling people, and God is greatly using him. And he's not administrating much of anything.

How do you help your volunteers find their sweet spots? Here are some suggestions:

1. *Learn about people first through a personal interview.* Private, personal recruitment is so important! It gives you an opportunity to interview prospective workers and learn

as much as you can about them before you suggest a position for them.

2. *Establish a trial period.* This takes the personal offense out of a situation if you have to move someone. For example, say, "Let's try you out in [you name the position], and then let's talk about it in two months. At that point, you can tell me if you think it is a good fit for the way God has wired you, and I'll also tell you what I've observed."

3. *Use a spiritual gifts assessment*—or even a personality assessment—as a tool to help determine where people might fit in ministry.

4. *Raise the question.* Are you in your sweet spot? It's something you should be asking at least on an annual basis. I know I'm happiest and most productive in ministry when I am in mine, and I'm sure you are, too. Your workers are no different.

5. *Create a position.* You may need to adapt your program to the gifts of your people, rather than try to fit them into your program. Said another way, instead of trying to fit a square peg into a round hole, create some square holes!

The Harvest

A second thing that gives personal meaning to ministry is the privilege of participating in the harvest.

For several years in a row, we took our grandkids to a farm in late October to experience harvest time. Since they lived in a suburb, they really hadn't thought much about how you picked apples, or shucked corn, or found the best pumpkin. One year, they got completely carried away picking apples (okay, so maybe it was me, too). We got a bag and ended up stuffing it so full we had enough apples for the whole winter.

Picking apples is not a spectator sport. There's very little joy in just watching others pick them—the satisfaction comes when you participate in the harvest yourself. It's a *little* different in ministry, because there *is* joy in observing others reap a harvest. When a co-worker has the privilege of leading a student to Christ, *I* rejoice. I'm sure you do, too. But just like with picking apples, it's even more satisfying when I can participate in the harvest. And just as it is true for me, it is true for others as well. I have too easily forgotten that at times.

As a ministry leader, I confess I have relished having the roles of Chief Advice Giver and Master Question Answerer. It has certainly stroked my ego to be the High Exalted Authority of Biblical Interpretation as well. Seriously, no one has ever *given* me those titles, but I recognize I have usurped those positions at times. As I have gotten older, I have learned that when I hang on to those roles too tightly, I cheat someone else out of the opportunity to grow and to serve.

Here's your job, ministry leader: Allow as many workers as you can to participate in as much of the harvest as possible. When they are able to do that, they will find more personal meaning in ministry and stay more faithful. Here are three things you can do:

Assign Each Worker a Small Group of Children or Students as Their Responsibility

Don't let anyone off the hook—the secretary, the teenager who just comes in to play the guitar for worship, or the "helper" who does all the behind-the-scenes stuff. If nothing else, encourage them to pray regularly for those assigned to them and to express godly love to them at every opportunity. When workers see *people* rather than a *task* as their responsibility, they will be much more focused on a spiritual harvest.

Share the Opportunity to Counsel

Some ministry leaders keep this important role for themselves because they feel they can do it best—and they may be right. But in doing so, they deny their workers the opportunity to experience some of the greatest blessings of ministry. Think about my earlier story of Shelly and Pastor John. What if he had told the children, "If you want to understand better about becoming a Christian, come talk to *me*?" He probably would have done it better (or at least in a more experienced and confident way), but the two men would have quit. Let me paint a scenario:

Scenario	Questions
1. I'm teaching a Senior High group on Sunday morning. The lesson is on giving God's grace to others. At the end, I tell the students, "If God is speaking to you about your need to be more gracious, and you want someone to pray with you about it, I will stay up front here, and I will talk to you if you want." After I pray, three guys come to the front and share their situations with me. I spend time counseling them and answering their questions.	What are the other workers doing while I am counseling the three guys? How personally involved do they feel with those three?
2. Same situation, but at the end, I tell them, "If you want someone to pray with you, come up to the front, and I will see that someone talks to you if you want." After I pray, three guys come to the front. As they share their situations, I ask three workers to each talk and pray with one of the guys.	How much more involved in the ministry will my people feel if I take this approach? How will the ministry be benefited? What precautions do you need to take?

Point Out the Wins

Ron Hughey, a children's pastor in Michigan, says he does this regularly to keep his people energized and committed. As a ministry leader, you have to look for spiritual victories yourself, ask others to watch for them, and then encourage the workers and the children to share them. Then, when you find them, you celebrate them with everyone. When there is the sense that you are always in "harvest mode," your workers will be more motivated to be faithful.

Growth Spurts

A third thing that gives personal meaning in ministry is experiencing a personal spiritual growth spurt.

My grandson, Travis, is twelve, and of course he is in the middle of a major physical growth spurt. Every time we see him, he's visibly taller, and he loves it when we notice.

Just like children, we get excited when we grow. Of course we're done growing taller, and I'm not talking about growing horizontally—we're usually not too excited about that. But we love it when we have a *spiritual* growth spurt.

That describes my spiritual life pretty well—growth spurts. I'll cruise along for a while with a slow but steady rate of growth; then sometimes, I'm embarrassed to admit, I go backwards. But then there will come The Spurt. Maybe there's a new subject I've become immersed in, or a truth I have more fully discovered. Maybe it comes as a result of a conference, or a message, or my own personal study, but however it begins, The Spurt propels me forward in my following of Christ. This is what happened when I first discovered this passage in Nehemiah and began to understand the implications of his leadership.

I've discovered that this kind of growth also happens when people work with kids. I've taught the subject of this book on many occasions. I begin by asking my students, "Tell me what working in children's ministry means to you *personally*." It's very predictable—the answers are nearly always a version of "I have grown spiritually myself because I have been involved in ministry."

So here's a question for you to think about: How many of your workers are growing spiritually through their service? All ministry leaders want their volunteers to grow spiritually, but we tend to compartmentalize—go to the worship service and/or small groups to grow; work with children and youth to serve. Here's my premise: Service *itself* must be a part of the spiritual growth process. I believe it usually is, but we often fail to point it out or challenge our team members to see it that way.

How can you be more active in guiding your workers to grow spiritually themselves? Here are some suggestions:

1. *Encourage them to model* whatever the children or teens are asked to do. Do you ask them to memorize a Bible verse every week? Expect your volunteers to do the same.

2. *Emphasize preparation.* Say something like this, "If you don't put your heart into preparation, you are cheating yourself—because it is the preparation of the lesson that benefits you and causes you to grow."

3. *Recognize those who do.* That's the next point, so I won't elaborate on it here.

Appreciation

A fourth way to make ministry personally meaningful is to provide plenty of genuine, heartfelt appreciation.

Everyone likes to be appreciated. Have you ever connected the two main meanings of this word? To appreciate in financial terms means to gain value; to appreciate in personal terms means to recognize worth. When you recognize the worth of your volunteers (appreciation), they gain value (appreciation). And the more they feel personally valued, the more personal meaning they find in their ministry. You want your workers to feel essential to the ministry—like each is the central hub of the wheel, the vital link in the chain.

But *how* do you help workers feel that valued? Most of us show appreciation according to who *we* are, but we must develop skill sets that enable us to demonstrate it according to who our workers are.

Gifts

I am certain it is not news to you that you can show appreciation with gifts. Lindsey Woods, from Missouri, says, "Any excuse we have, we try to give little thank-you gifts to our workers. We distribute holiday gifts. We personally write thank-you notes to let them know that we appreciate them. We feed them any time we have training. And we try to affirm what they do even with email." Do you attempt to do the same? Regularly? As Lindsey says, for "any excuse"?

Bill Gunter of Pennsylvania does the same: "I gave personal handwritten thank-you notes to everyone who participated in children's ministry, thanking them for how they specifically served in the previous year and how it was a blessing."

Greg Braly, from Minnesota, says, "We find simple ways to thank our people throughout the year. It could be with a superhero gift card for a free donut at our café, or just notes and cards."

Titles

Some volunteers find value in the title they have. You hear it negatively expressed when someone says, "I'm *just* a _____ [fill in the blank]." Titles can help provide focus and direction in what people do. For example, your Sunday morning workers—what are they called? Think about what term you use. Could people feel more important if you gave them a special title? I'm not talking about making it ridiculous, like Chief Exalted Chair Setter-Upper. I encourage you to make every title have a ministry focus. So you have someone set up chairs? Make them part of the Ministry Environment Team—maybe they will go beyond just setting up chairs and do other things to enhance the environment for ministry.

Greg (see above) says, "Our fifth- and sixth-grade students involved in a service team are called DOGS—Disciples of God in Service. Our fourth- to sixth-grade prayer team, which is made up of kids trained to be prayer warriors—we call them 'Hope Watchers.'"

Recognition

Consider using awards to encourage your people. Have an appreciation dinner, and if you can handle it time-wise, recognize *every* single one of them. Take time to think through what you can give awards for. Here are some ideas:

1. *Teacher of the Year*. Why *not* choose one—or five—or ten? You will honor them, and some others (don't expect

all) will aspire to that honor in future years. Michael Lacy, from Ohio, does a "Hall of Fame" for his workers. He uses it to recognize those who excel over an extended period of time.

2. *Fruit of the Spirit Awards.* In other words, hand out the "Love Award," the "Joy Award," the "Longsuffering Award," etc. This approach recognizes workers' godly character more than external achievements.

3. *Individual Actions Awards.* For example, "Best Lesson of the Year" award, "Most Counted Upon to Be on Time" award, or . . .

4. *Useful Awards.* Your adults are not likely to put a plaque you give them on a wall. So whatever categories of recognition you choose, consider making the award something more useful: a gift card, for example. Alternatively, you can put the award title on a corsage or boutonniere for the evening. The recognition is far more important than the physical award.

Here's an important tip to remember about giving out awards: It's critical that you think through what you will say about each person receiving one. How deeply your people feel appreciated is in direct proportion to the careful thought you put into what you say about them. For example, if you were to give out Fruit of the Spirit awards, and can cite specific examples of why you gave the "Joy Award" to a certain person, the award is validated and becomes a real source of encouragement. Without specific examples and careful thought, the value of the award diminishes.

Special Treatment
Your volunteers work hard to ensure that the children or others they serve have a positive experience in your ministry program. Your efforts to make your workers' experience enjoyable and in-

teresting will go a long way toward keeping them enthusiastic about their involvement. Jane Larson, a ministry friend from Iowa, gives these ideas:

- We would try to read a current children's storybook during our teacher training times. When we did, I would have one copy per table to give away—who got the book would vary each time. For example, it might be the person who was newest to the children's ministry, or the person with the most children under his or her care, and so forth.

- We gave out certificates for their classes, such as FREE doughnuts and juice to be served to their class by the pastor. Or a certificate could be good for one class session in any odd location of the church (baptismal, pastors office, and so on). Kids *loved* these perks, and the variation from the routine encouraged creativity and memorable moments!

- One time I had a limo pick up the teachers in groups and take them for breakfast and back. We had two limos running for two hours . . . it was GREAT! They loved it!

Veronica Culberson, from Kansas, adds this: "We have taken [our workers] on a 'mystery trip,' as well as a brunch at Christmas time. We have also done 'The Price Is Right' with silly prizes . . . it's always a big hit!"

Words

Don't forget—your words are powerful tools of appreciation, too. Like giving gifts, this is not a new revelation. But I've found that many ministry leaders haven't learned the skill of *how* to express appreciation. Following are some thoughts that have been very helpful to me.

Somewhere along the way, you've likely taken some sort of personality test. If so, you have learned to recognize four different personality styles. There are many different forms of personality differentiation, some Christian and some secular. Pastor Tim La-Haye resurrected and popularized Galen's[1] four personality styles several decades ago and called them the Four Spiritual Temperaments. More recently, Christian marriage and family expert Dr. Gary Smalley has used animal designations to make personality styles easier to remember. Many businesses use the popular DISC Personality Profile. In the training I am responsible for developing in Awana, we refer to the different personality types with colors.[2] In the rest of this section I'll use those color designations with which I'm familiar. We can chart the four styles this way:

D (Dominance) *Choleric* Lion Red	I (Influence) *Sanguine* Otter Blue
C (Conscientiousness) *Phlegmatic* Beaver Yellow	S (Steadiness) *Melancholic* Golden Retriever Green

In this matrix, the top two quadrants are the more extroverted styles; the bottom two are more introverted. The left two personality styles are more task-oriented, while the right two are more people-oriented. No matter what we call them, these categories can help us to understand how people prefer to be shown appreciation. While most of us are grateful for appreciation in any form, we certainly have preferences about how it is delivered.

Ministry leaders tend to express appreciation according to their own personality styles, rather than taking into consideration their workers' styles. Therefore:

- Red (D) leaders tend to not do it very often; they wait for a compelling reason. They think, "When you do something really significant, then I'll tell you I appreciate you."

- Blue (I) ministry leaders tend to do it publicly and pour on the praise. They may exaggerate or do it so often that it loses meaning.

- Green (S) ministry leaders will tell you privately but are reluctant to make a big deal out of it. They will focus on what you mean to them.

- Yellow (C) ministry leaders will acknowledge effort and quality. They tend to focus more on the work than on the person.

So, how do different workers *react* to appreciation? The following chart illustrates how the personality styles generally respond to four different approaches to demonstrating appreciation. The shaded areas show the best approach for each personality:

	Success is recognized	Public applause	Private appreciation	Work is acknowledged
The Red person thinks:	Prefers this—wants the results to show.	"Just give me the plaque so I can get out of here."	"You're not going to hug me, are you?"	"Forget the details, just get to the point."
The Blue person thinks:	"Don't stop! Go on …and on …"	Prefers this—wants people to know.	"Wait, I want all my friends to hear this."	"Okay, but how wonderful do you think I am?"
The Green person thinks:	"You must not like me. You only talked about what I did."	"This is embarrassing."	Prefers this—wants to know your words are heart-felt.	"I had lots of help. You need to recognize others, too."
The Yellow person thinks:	"Of course I got it done. But did you like the way I did it?"	"Don't get mushy on me or exaggerate."	"You're getting too close—just tell me if my work was good."	Prefers this—wants quality to be noticed.

As a ministry leader, learn to show appreciation to others according to the way God wired them. For example, if you are an extrovert who is task oriented (according to our system, Red), think about how you can make your appreciation more personal for your worker who is Green. If you are Blue, you will want to shower praise publicly on your workers, but Yellows and Greens may want it done more privately.

	Task-Focused	**Person-focused**
Public	**D** (Red) Likes recognition of tasks completed	**I** (Blue) Likes public applause
Private	**C** (Yellow) Likes recognition of quality work	**S** (Green) Likes private appreciation

A Final Exercise

Think about each of your volunteers. It may be helpful even to make a list of them (you likely have an email or phone directory) and go through it. Ask yourself these questions:

1. Is this person finding personal meaning in how they are serving?
2. If the answer is yes, then "How?"
3. If the answer is no, then "How can I help this person find personal meaning?"
4. If the answer is "I don't know," then "How can I find out?"

Your JOB, ministry leader, is to help your workers find that personal meaning. Be like Nehemiah and make it happen!

Think and Talk About It

1. Have you personally grown spiritually through your ministry involvement? Think about each of the following and describe your experience: (1) the sweet spot, (2) the harvest, and (3) the growth spurt.

2. How do you react to the idea that workers are much more likely to stay involved if they find personal meaning in their ministry?

3. Think about your workers. Who do you believe is really finding personal fulfillment and satisfaction in their service?

4. Who do you think is in the "danger zone" of putting out and putting out but never receiving?

5. Think about your workers. To whom have you made a specific effort to show appreciation in the past three months?

6. Whom have you overlooked?

7. If you have overlooked anyone, what will you do about it?

8. Look at the section on personality styles as they relate to words of appreciation. Can you think of members of your team who exhibit each personality style? How might you express appreciation differently to each?

Notes
1. Claudius Galenus, also known as Galen, was a second-century Roman physician.
2. The column designations are based on the DISC Personality Profile; the designations "Choleric," "Sanguine," "Phlegmatic" and "Melancholic" were popularized by Dr. Tim LaHaye; the designations "Lion," "Otter," "Beaver" and "Golden Retriever" were developed by Dr. Gary Smalley; and the colors "Red," "Blue," "Yellow" and "Green" are used in Awana training.

EQUIP FOR WORK, EQUIP FOR WAR

From that day on, half of my men did the work, while the other half were equipped with spears, shields, bows and armor. The officers posted themselves behind all the people of Judah who were building the wall. Those who carried materials did their work with one hand and held a weapon in the other, and each of the builders wore his sword at his side as he worked.
NEHEMIAH 4:16-18

Uzziel here again.

We received some disturbing news today. Four travelers—fellow Jews—came through from the east. They were Ephraimites on their way home to Shiloh. They said they had been down to Ezion-Geber and had come back north on the eastern side of the Dead Sea, near the border of Ammon. They came through Jerusalem because they had heard about Nehemiah and our work on the wall and wanted to warn us before they went on home.

The spokesman was a short man, about 40, with bushy hair and a huge beard. He hadn't trimmed it at all, and his beard came so high up on his cheeks that it nearly hid his eyes. The smell of camels was all over him, and one look at his clothes made it clear that he had been on a long, dirty journey. As several of us workers gathered around him, he saw a log nearby and stepped up on it so people could see and hear him better.

"There was a lot of activity in Ammon," he said. "The people there told us that their leaders were forcing men into the army and saying that now was the time to attack Jerusalem—before it gets too fortified. We thought Nehemiah ought to know."

He went on to tell us that he had seen stashes of weapons and corrals full of horses, as if the Ammonites were getting staged to come fight. He had seen women packing food into bundles, too. All that he told us certainly seemed to indicate that the enemy was coming.

A second traveler in the group had an Ammonite sword and was showing it around. I got to see it—I even held it for a little bit. I was really impressed; it was the sharpest sword I have ever seen. Of course, we haven't had too many swords around here in recent years ...

I said I was impressed, but really it was more than that. I was scared—scared a lot. Through the rest of the day, I couldn't make my mind erase the image of that sword. We'd been working on the wall with tools we had found, or tools that we used in our businesses. Some of us had hammers and chisels to chip the stones into a shape that would fit in the wall. Others had trowels to put the mortar in the cracks. But none of us had anything like that sword, or anything that could stop a sword like that if we were attacked.

I had been feeling pretty good, being able to work with my family and all. But this report about Ammon frankly left me weak-kneed. The real possibility of an attack was all I could think about. What if they were on their way now? Would we survive? What if our work on the wall had angered them so much that they—and the Arabs and the Samarians and the Ashdodites—attacked us before we could be ready to defend ourselves?

The feelings of wanting to just quit and get out of here with my wife and three little boys returned ... BIG time ...

Ministry Is Work *and* War

Ministry can be described as work. It is work—*hard* work! In fact, throughout the New Testament, it is often described that way. Paul told Timothy that the purpose of Scripture was "that the man of God may be thoroughly equipped for every good work" (2 Tim. 3:17). We are called God's workers in 1 Corinthians 3:9, hardworking farmers in 2 Timothy 2:6, and workmen in 2 Timothy 2:15. According to Ephesians 2:10, we are created in Christ Jesus to do good works. Ministry is *work*.

But it can just as accurately be described as *war*. Paul also told Timothy, commenting on his own ministry, "I have fought the good fight" (2 Tim. 4:7). We are called soldiers in 2 Timothy 2:3, told to put on the armor of God in Ephesians 6:11, and instructed to fight in 1 Timothy 1:18.

Nehemiah saw the need to equip his volunteers for both aspects of ministry. At the beginning, the workers needed to be equipped with tools for rebuilding the wall; but as the threats increased, they also needed to be equipped to repel the enemy.

We're not told how he got the swords and spear and bows, but he did. Maybe some were already in Jerusalem. That's not too likely—they had been, and still were, under the rule of foreign kings. Most occupied peoples aren't allowed to have military capabilities. Maybe Nehemiah brought weapons with him—we just don't know.

What we do know is that he saw the need to equip his workers for the work—and for the war—and he did both.

The Work of the Ministry

You are probably familiar with the ministry progression revealed in Ephesians 4:11-13, but look at it with me:

And He Himself gave some to be apostles, some prophets, some evangelists, and some pastors and teachers, for the equipping of the saints for the work of ministry, for the edifying of the body of Christ, till we all come to the unity of the faith and of the knowledge of the Son of God, to a perfect man, to the measure of the stature of the fullness of Christ (*NKJV*).

Where are you in this progression? If you are like me, you'd say, "I'm at every level." True, we all are at every level. I'm a leader and a worker; I'm involved in serving; I'm part of the Body and in the process of becoming mature. But in your role as a ministry leader, your Ephesians 4 responsibility is to equip the workers for their works of service.

I'm not much of a mechanic, but I do know how to change brake pads. Usually, it means taking off a tire, taking out two bolts, replacing the old pads with new ones, and then putting things back together. The last time I had to do it, I had waited too long. The pads had worn down to nothing, and as a result the rotors (the shiny discs that the pads clamp down on when you put on the brakes) were scratched and had to be replaced too. This meant more work; now I had to take out four bolts, not two.

Not a big deal, huh? Well, it *was*: The two additional bolts were on the back side of the wheel hub, still factory-tightened, and I think a little rusted as well. I didn't have the right tools to apply enough leverage to loosen them. Besides that, my wrench wasn't exactly the right size, and it kept slipping. After over an hour of getting sore muscles and bruised and cut knuckles, I was almost ready to give up and take it into a shop. But I'm stubborn, so I decided instead to try to get a better tool. At the third auto-parts store, I found just what I needed—a longer, sturdier wrench that was just the right size. I returned home, and I had the rotor off in about three minutes. It was a perfect illustration of the importance of having the right tool!!

Finding the Right Tools

There's another aspect of my brake rotor adventure that I want you to notice: At first, I didn't *know* that I needed a different tool. I thought that what I had would do. Only after an hour of frustration and no success did I finally wake up to the fact that a better tool was what I needed.

I've said about the topics in the previous chapters, "Ministry leader, this is your job!" Well—your job's not done yet: Another *critical* aspect of your role as a leader is to make sure that your workers have the tools they need. But—what do they need? *They* often don't even know.

Why *don't* they know? There are several possible reasons:

1. *They aren't focused on the right thing.* We already talked about this in Motivation 3, but here's what I mean in this context: If our workers are focused on the kids simply staying occupied, it may be that a video is all they need for a tool. Why would they need training—or equipment—beyond that? But if they are focused on building a foundation of God's truth into the kids they work with, that immediately prompts the question, "So how do we do that?" And the need for ministry tools becomes an issue.

2. *They don't know it can be different.* Remember my brake rotor replacement story above? I'll never again try to replace a rotor with the wrong wrench, because I found out how *different* the task is when I have the right tool. When it comes to ministry, our workers often don't know it can be different either. When kids are out of control, they think that's just the way kids are. When the children's attention is everywhere but on the lesson, they accept it—if that's all they have experienced. So often our ministry leaders are not exposed to new ideas or other ways of doing things. Let me suggest something: Find a sister church—or two or three—and take your workers to go observe their ministries. Yes, it is a lot of work to find substitutes for that week, arrange transportation, and so forth, but the effort will yield great benefits for your workers. They will learn

by seeing different approaches, better or not, and will come back energized.

3. *They aren't aware of the enemy.* Who needs weapons for war when the enemy isn't close or threatening? You're probably familiar with 1 Peter 5:8: "Be self-controlled and alert. Your enemy the devil prowls around like a roaring lion looking for someone to devour." Is this warning still relevant today? It is, but many of us are unaware of the danger. Part of your responsibility as a leader is to help your workers understand the nature of the opposition they face, and then supply them with what they need to confront those threats.

I'm beyond the parenting years now. I consider myself a young grandparent, but still—my peers are people whose children aren't grown. A number of them have seen the enemy "steal" their kids' hearts away from the things of God. In several cases, the tool Satan used was materialism or even hedonism; for others, the devil has lured them through a different belief system. Mark and Tonya (not their real names) are an example: Only one of their three sons is currently following God. The other two have given them incredible grief, countless sleepless nights, and deep disappointment. But Mark and Tonya are turning their pain and heartache into something good. They have a passion for young parents and are trying to warn, encourage and instruct them so that they will be more intentional in raising their children spiritually.

Do *you* know what the tools for ministry work are? It's pretty easy to figure out when the job is a physical one:

- The floor is dirty—you need a broom or a mop.
- The brake pads need changing—you need the right-sized wrench.
- The wall needs building—you need trowels to put the mortar in the cracks.

It's a lot harder when the work is spiritual. These are the kinds of questions we need to answer as we engage in ministry:

- How do you shepherd children?
- How do you help them grow spiritually?
- How do you bring about heart change in your students?
- What do your workers need in their ministry tool bag?

The next section will describe my four most critical tools for the work of the ministry with children and youth.

Equipping for Work

Ministry is more art than science, and there's certainly no formula that guarantees a certain outcome if you perform certain actions. Nevertheless, through my own experience and the experience of trusted ministry friends, I've learned that using the tools we're about to discuss greatly increases your likelihood of having a positive aspect on those you serve.

Tool #1: A Discipline System

A discipline system is more than a set of classroom rules. It includes a chain of command, clear policy about follow-up, unified techniques implemented throughout the ministry, and yes, rules for the children and youth workers as well.

1. *The chain of command.* This means that within your ministry, you and your workers know who handles what problem. On one occasion, I was guiding a small group of fifth- and sixth-grade boys in my church. Actually, on that particular day the group wasn't so small, because I had three visitors, and my regular group of six boys had swelled to nine. We were all seated around a table; I was in the middle of one side of the table, and I was working with the guys to my right. I wasn't aware that two boys at the other end had started insulting

each other with racial remarks. Startled by a sudden commotion, I turned to see these two start to get up, and their tempers were *hot*. I knew fists would form soon if I didn't intervene, so I got involved in a hurry. Stopping the fight, however, was just the beginning of my responsibility; there was some heart work that needed to be done. At the same time, I had seven other boys there that needed my ministry as well. I was so glad that we had a clear chain of command already in place; I called the director over to my table, asked him to take the two boys, and he did. He did the heart work with them privately, and I was able to continue to work with the rest.

2. *Written policy.* This is for handling individual issues of misbehavior, especially those that are severe. Many ministries can go years without having a need for such a policy, but one severe incident that is mishandled can cause a successful ministry to come crashing down. Getting a policy in writing is preventative—put it in place before you need it, and it will guide you through a crisis and save you a lot of trouble, legal and otherwise.

3. *Unified techniques.* We frustrate our students with inconsistent approaches to discipline. Kids are allowed to do something in one session, and then chastised for the same behavior in another—this only results in confusion and de-motivation. Taking the time upfront to make sure all your workers are on the same page, and everyone knows what to expect, will result in fewer headaches later on.

4. *Clear rules.* Not too many, worded positively, communicated clearly, and if necessary, posted for everyone to see.

Tool #2: Structure

I remember visiting a church in Bakersfield, California, with a large (and growing) children's ministry. Their program for preschoolers amazed me; there were about 100 children in the ministry, and all of them seemed so calm and happy. It was so *orderly*. I wasn't sure what the secret was, but it didn't change the fact that I was impressed. I later asked the director to teach a workshop on discipline (because that is what I observed was so good) for a conference I was administering. Her answer was memorable: "I don't know if I can do that. I don't know what I would say, because we really haven't had any discipline problems." I thought, *No discipline problems? You've got a hundred preschoolers. How can you have no discipline problems?*

As we conversed, I realized that the reason she had very few discipline problems was because of her exceptional effort to have a clear structure that all of her workers understood. It was flexible, but there was always something to hold the attention of the children. I changed my request; I asked her to teach on organization and administration, and she agreed. Her workshop was fantastic. I felt it was still about discipline, though—her work to have a highly organized program resulted not only in a smooth-running ministry, but also in a very small number of discipline issues.

Structure is a *tool*. It is never the goal, but a means to an end. It is easy, especially in our Western culture, to get the two confused. Sometimes people see structure as constricting—as a hindrance, rather than a benefit. I believe many people who see it that way do so because they have experienced its misuse; they've been in situations where structure became the goal, rather than the means.

I've also observed ministries that could really use structure. Our Awana Clubs use a game time to draw unchurched children, and this strategy is hugely effective all around the world. It is meant to be highly structured, but that doesn't mean all who do it follow the plan. I recently observed this in one club: The game director would introduce a new game by gathering the other leaders into a small circle, explaining the rules and answering questions. What do you think the kids were doing for the two or three

minutes while that was going on? Whatever they wanted! So by
the time the leaders were finished getting the instructions, the kids
were out of control. Then the director had his hands more than
full trying to get their cooperation. The whole problem came from
a lack of structure.

Structure does not have to be militant; it can be very flexible.
But it assures that something intentional is happening and that
workers are united in making it happen. It simply means that
everyone understands what to do and when to do it.

Ministries *need* structure. Does yours have it? Do your workers
have a clear understanding of what to do and when to do it? If
your answer is yes, then you've got structure. This is one way you
equip your people to fulfill their ministry task in an efficient, God-
honoring way.

Tool #3: Ministry Skills

What a huge category! There are teaching skills, technical skills,
counseling skills, theatrical skills, organizational skills, leadership
skills—and that's just the beginning of the list. It goes without saying that the more skills your workers have, the more effective they
will be in ministry. I'm not about to tackle all of the skills that can
be useful in ministry; I want to focus on what I consider to be the
most important skills for working with kids. Here are my Top Five
Ministry Skills:

1. The Skill of Loving

I agonize over calling this a skill; after all, it is first and foremost
a heart issue. However, I have observed many children and youth
workers struggle with showing it. So, I can't leave it off my list. In
fact, it is so critical that I rate it my number one skill.

First Corinthians 13 is thought of as the Love Chapter, but it
is more than that; it is also the Serve Chapter. At the end of chapter 12's discussion of spiritual gifts—given for the purpose of serving the Body—the apostle Paul says, "And now I will show you the
most excellent way" (1 Cor. 12:31). Way to do what? To *serve*. Then,
the first three verses of chapter 13 list exemplary ways of serving,

and compare each one with love. This chart will help illustrate what I am saying:

Exemplary service	Beyond amazing service	But without love ...
Speak in the tongues of men	And of angels	I am only a sounding gong
Gift of prophecy	Fathom all mysteries and all knowledge	I am nothing
Have faith	Faith that can move mountains	I am nothing
Give all I possess to the poor	Surrender my body to the flames	I gain nothing

Think about the first column. If you had a volunteer who could do those things, wouldn't you be excited? You'd be talking about this person all the time. What about one who could do the things in the middle column? You'd just about die for a volunteer like that, wouldn't you? But Paul says that kind of a servant—that kind of a volunteer—is worth nothing if he or she doesn't love.

Do you see? Love is the *best* way to serve! Then Paul helps us understand what love looks like. You're very familiar with these, I am sure, but I want to remind you that the following verses paint a wonderful picture of how to love—and how not to love:

> Love is patient, love is kind. It does not envy, it does not boast, it is not proud. It is not rude, it is not self-seeking, it is not easily angered, it keeps no record of wrongs. Love does not delight in evil but rejoices with the truth. It always protects, always trusts, always hopes, always perseveres (1 Cor. 13:4-7).

I can *say* I love the kids I am ministering to, but when I get angry easily, I lose my ability to minister. When I am impatient, or self-seeking, or not protective—or anything else on this list—I fail to minister to my students. First Peter 4:8 tells us, "Love covers over a multitude of sins." It also covers a lot of other inadequacies in a ministry worker.

2. The Skill of Asking Questions

It's significant that Jesus' primary tools in influencing people were asking questions and telling stories. In children's ministry, we are too often tempted to tell, rather than to ask. In fact, most of us in children's ministry are better advice-givers than we are question-askers. After all, we *know so much more* than the kids. If they would only listen to us . . . Know what I mean?

We know it is possible that we can say the right things, and yet children don't learn them. It is also possible that children can learn the right facts, but their thinking doesn't change. It's easier to evaluate our ministries by *what we say* than by *what they learn*. It is even more difficult to go beyond what kids learn and evaluate what they are thinking. Yet, that is the target of ministry: to change how people think so it is in agreement with God's Word. The Bible portrays the heart as the center of thinking, and that should be our target.

> Most of us in children's ministry are better advice-givers than we are question askers.

When we ask the right kind of question, we discover what kids are thinking. We need to ask "Why?" and "How?" questions, or any other type that encourages thought. I probably don't need to remind you that the questions have to be on an appropriate age level.

Diane and I enjoy the friendship of Chuck and Winnie Christensen, who have spent a lifetime in ministry leadership. They are 80 but have the health and energy of 40-year-olds. Winnie teaches middle elementary girls in our church, and she recently asked them, "What do you want to be when you are 80?"

She enjoyed relating to us their answers. I thought her question was a great one: It made the girls think past the typical career-choice answer that comes when someone asks a kid, "What do you want to be when you grow up?"

When we ask the right kind of question, we follow Jesus' model. My good friend Dr. Greg Carlson says the following in his book *Rock-Solid Teacher*:

> *Learning the skill of asking the right questions on an age-appropriate level is one of the best ways to influence thinking.*

During Jesus' most intense leadership-development times with the disciples, He used rhetorical questions: "What good is it for a man to gain the whole world, and yet lose or forfeit his very self?" (Luke 9:25). He didn't expect the disciples to answer; He was trying to jumpstart their thinking. Even when He was on trial, Jesus sought to teach by clarifying and deepening His judge's opinion: "'Is that your own idea,' Jesus asked, 'or did others talk to you about me?'" (John 18:34). Jesus used questions to clarify priorities, get others to think and evaluate information, all for the overarching purpose of increasing people's knowledge of God.[1]

Learning the skill of asking the right questions on an age-appropriate level is one of the best ways to influence thinking. So—how do you ask the right questions? First, know what kind of answer you want. If you are satisfied with simple, factual answers, the questions are pretty easy. But if you want to probe what your students are thinking, then you need different questions. You can judge your question-asking by the answers your students give you. If they are simply regurgitating facts, then you didn't ask the right questions. Here are some practical tips:

- *Dig deeper.* To get at what they really think, ask questions like, "Why do you think that is true?" "What do you think caused that?" "Can you explain that?"

- *Make connections.* This is especially important in studying Scripture. Look for opportunities to ask, "Can you think of any other Bible character that did that?" "Can you think of another place where we are told that?" "How do you know that?"

- *Consider consequences.* Help them to consider the future by asking, "What might happen if I didn't listen to that?" "How might this hurt me or others?"

- *Seek another perspective.* Help them to consider the values and viewpoints of others: "How do you think [your parents, your school friends, your pastor] would answer this question?"

Most of these questions, with some modifications, will work across most age groups. It is, of course, easier as children get older and can think abstractly, but it is possible even with small children. My opinion is that this skill is especially critical to effectively work with teens.

3. The Skill of Listening

My wife, Diane, is an incredible listener. I'm the talker in our marriage, and she complements me perfectly. I confess that way too often when she is talking, I'm trying to listen and also think about something else at the same time. But when I talk, she gives me her best attention. It is one of the reasons that I appreciate her so much! Needless to say, the kids she works with as a volunteer love her as well, in part because she shows genuine interest in them through how she *listens.*

Why is listening so important? Because it is how we know what is going on in the minds and the hearts of our students. Yet, I'm persuaded that in many children's and youth ministries, we aren't listening well to them. We love to teach them. We get positive strokes when they listen to us, but we forget how valuable it is to our relationship with them when we are the listeners. Remember that James 1:19 tells us, "My dear brothers, take note of this: Everyone should be quick to listen, slow to speak and slow to become angry."

To help your workers to be good listeners, you need to . . .

- *Set aside time in your ministry structure for it.* Most youth groups have time scheduled for kids to hang out, and that gives their adult leaders an opportunity to interact and listen. But in children's ministry, time for listening is often overlooked. It can be pre-meeting time, or post-meeting refreshments, or in small groups, but we should include time to listen.

> Listening is how we know what is going on in the minds and hearts of our students.

- *Organize to allow for it.* Listening to the hearts of our kids doesn't usually happen before there is a relationship connection; in other words, the kids will need to trust before they let the adult worker hear their thoughts. That means (1) a worker needs to have the same group from week to week; (2) the worker needs to be consistent in attendance; and (3) small groups need to be small enough to allow for significant personal interaction.

- *Train for it.* Practice listening skills, talk about how important it is to hear what your students are thinking, relate stories of ministry successes that have come through listening (without betraying confidences, of course), and generally remind your workers how vital this approach is.

4. The Skill of Age Appropriateness

Have you ever seen a ministry fail because the workers weren't using age-appropriate materials or methods? I have. I have also seen many struggle. Most workers are comfortable with one age group, but afraid of another. The really skilled worker can adapt his or her teaching to whatever age group is in the room at the time.

I once visited a church in the Los Angeles area to evaluate their club ministry. When the director met me, I asked him if there were any frustrations he had that I might be able to help with. He told me, "I can't get the other workers to stay in the room during the large group time. If you can help me figure out what to do, I'd appreciate that." I promised him I would. When the large group time came, I was a little surprised, because he had all the kids come in together—three-year-olds through sixth-graders, all in one group. The club was pretty large, given the size of the church, and it could—and should—have been divided. There were probably 150 children in the room. The director was right about the workers—quite a few left, and those that stayed hung around in the back. I could see he had a *problem!* As he started the session, I quickly understood why the workers were reluctant to be in there: He was the teacher, and they were avoiding his teaching. His one visual was a flip chart, with probably 10 lines of text written from edge to edge. No pictures, nothing except words—and there were lots of them, and they were big ones.

I still remember his subject matter: He was teaching Campus Crusade's materials on how to be filled with the Holy Spirit. To *kids*—three-year-olds even! The students were bored beyond belief. The little ones couldn't sit still, and the older ones weren't paying attention. It was *painful* just to sit in there. I could understand why the rest of the adults didn't want to be there. The director thought *they* were the problem. Later, I shared the truth with him—that his teaching style and the content of his lesson were not age-appropriate. To his credit, he listened to what I told him. I didn't come back to see if he changed, but not long after that, he left to work in another ministry. I hope it was a college-level program, because he would have been a good teacher there. He just didn't possess the skill of age appropriateness. He hadn't learned how to adapt his style.

Do you see? The lack of age appropriateness would have killed the ministry if he had continued.

5. The Skill of Counseling Someone Regarding Salvation

Why is it so critical to train children's workers and youth workers to counsel in this area? Here are three reasons:

First, *the childhood years are the greatest window of opportunity for sharing the gospel with a person.* The teen years are just behind them as far as opportunity goes. The super-majority of people who trust in Christ do so between the ages of 4 and 18. Therefore, it only makes sense that those who work with that age group would be equipped to guide them in that eternally important decision.

Yet the opposite is true. I am persuaded that in the vast majority of churches, no training is even offered, to say nothing of being required, for this critical topic. It is not only true on the local church level; it is true also on a professional level. In my personal survey of major children's ministry and youth ministry conferences in the last 12 months, I've found that less than 1 percent of topics offered have to do with leading a child or teen to Christ. Conference directors avoid it. A friend of mine, who is a gifted and nationally recognized workshop presenter, offered to teach this topic at a major conference. When he suggested it, he later told me, there was an uncomfortable pause on the phone. Then the conference director literally said this: "I don't think that will work, [name of my friend]. It's just not sexy enough." Why? I don't understand. But I'm calling for that to change.

> The super-majority of peple who trust in Christ do so between ages 4 and 18. Therefore, it only makes sense that those who work with that age group would be equipped to guide them in that eternally important decision.

Second, *just as receptivity for the gospel is at its height during youth, so is the potential for deception or confusion.* When we offer no training, workers are left to use methods and skills that either they just picked up by observation or they thought up themselves. Unfortunately, our American church cultures have encouraged methods and practices that end up deceiving kids with a false sense of a relationship with Christ. Past generations (mine included) have been so anxious to count results that we include actions in the salvation process that have no biblical basis at all. We have asked kids to "come forward," "raise their hands," "repeat this prayer," and a host of other invitations that betray our own theology and mislead the kids. We use confusing phrases, such as "let Jesus come into your heart" or its gruesome twin, "give your heart to Jesus." Kids can go through years of uncertainty because they were told they were saved because they did some physical action, when they should have been taught that salvation is the result of responding by faith from the heart, as the Bible clearly tells us to do. Training in leading a child or teen to Christ is so critical because wrong directions can lead to students thinking they are believers when in reality they are not.

People recognize that children can get confused by all the explanations out there, and they are rightfully concerned. They respond to this concern in different ways. Some bar children's workers from explaining the gospel to the kids, saying, "We need to wait until they can understand." Some question whether younger children can even be saved. Some change their theology. Children, they say, have a God-consciousness and, with proper nurturing, will gradually grow in their relationship with Him. They deny the depravity of a child and that spiritual regeneration is based upon faith in Christ.

A better response is to train properly. Children and teens *can* respond to the gospel. They *can* place their faith in Christ. With careful, accurate explanations of biblical truth repeated over time, God's Spirit can and will do His work in their hearts and draw them to Him.

Third, *because it has the greatest consequences*. Don't lose sight of the length of *eternity*. One measure of the significance of something is "How *long* will the impact last?" Something that has a brief impact—say, 80 years brief—has limited significance. But something that has *eternal* impact is infinitely more significant. I believe we are tempted to put more emphasis on training for the things we can see and neglect the things we can't, and that's not good. Children's ministry and youth workers, if they are skilled in anything at all, ought to be skilled in counseling a student to find Christ as Savior.

Tool #4: Incentives

A fourth tool workers need in their tool bags is an available repertoire of incentives.

When I was a boy, I had a competitive nature, but very little outlet for it. Growing up on a cattle ranch meant there was no Little League or any other organized sport. Even in my one-room country school there were only five kids (in the whole school), which made it nearly impossible to choose teams and play games during recess. So when I had a chance to be in a spelling competition, I was excited. Then I heard that the county champion got to go to a regional competition that was going to be on TV. *Me*—if I could win the county—*on TV!* The thought motivated me to begin studying like never before. My grandfather lived with us, and he would help me spell at least 1,000 words a night for several months before the contest. I never would have studied that much without the incentive of getting to be on TV if I won. Of course, at the time I never anticipated how proficiency in spelling would help me throughout my adult life—even in writing books. By the way, I did end up winning the county competition three years in a row, and got to be on TV each time!

Incentives are also helpful in ministering to kids. We all wish that children would intrinsically want to learn God's Word and grow as a disciple, but that's just not reality; they are too much like us adults! They need incentives . . . adults need incentives . . . *I* need incentives in my spiritual walk. Extrinsic help—incentives—can come in the form of a private word of encouragement; or an outing they can participate in as a privilege; or something tangible, like an award or gift. Be creative in coming up with incentives for the people you're ministering to; just remember that whatever they are, they need to be appropriate to the age of the student.

Kinds of Incentives

There are probably as many types of incentives as there are people who need to be motivated by them. Maybe you have some that you already use, or that you plan to use. Or maybe you're just getting started and haven't given much thought to how you might reward and encourage effort and excellence in your program. Wherever you are in the process, I hope you enjoy this part of your job—there's a lot of joy to be found both in celebrating the good things that are happening around you and laying the foundation for more good things to come.

Here are some general categories of incentives that I've found helpful over the years:

- *Personal affirmation.* The apostle Paul's pattern was to begin his letters to churches with personal affirmation. Can you imagine what it was like to be a member of the church in Thessalonica and have these words read to you: "We ought always to thank God for you, brothers, and rightly so, because your faith is growing more and more, and the love every one of you has for each other is increasing. Therefore, among God's churches we boast about your perseverance and faith in all the persecutions and trials you are enduring" (2 Thess. 1:3-4)? Personal affirmation usually takes the form of kind words privately spoken, but it can also occur in personal notes of appreciation (best if they are sent to the parents—that way you avoid child protection issues), happy faces, or any other indication that you are thankful for your students. A word of caution: Don't give personal gifts—that is a big child protection no-no.

- *Privileges.* Just getting to be the first small group dismissed to a large-group time can be huge! So can the opportunity to play a game, help a teacher, or have coffee with the pastor.

- *Leadership roles.* It's critical that these not be given out merely for a task completed. You don't want to undermine discipleship by allowing a student with an ungodly lifestyle to lead. At the same time, restless students may respond well to the challenge of leadership if accountability is made clear to them.

• *Special outings.* Outings, if they are things the students are really interested in doing together, can be huge incentives. I found one of the best was a "mystery trip." The intrigue was a factor, and I didn't have to have it planned until the last minute.

• *Public recognition.* Some of your kids will respond best to this kind of encouragement. Most of us (not all) like to be recognized in front of our peers, and a regular practice of doing this can help the whole group strive for right attitudes, cooperative responses, or anything else you feel is important for them to do.

• *Awards.* Awards are a part of life. We get awarded with good grades in school or raises at work. Kids get awards for athletic performance, music competitions, spelling bees (I've still got my ribbons in a box), and all sorts of other achievements. We all understand that those awards are not the end goal, but simply recognition of tasks completed or of excellence. In the same way, awards can serve as an incentive in ministries as well. In fact, I believe we may be sending the wrong message when kids get huge awards for participating on a sports team, but no award for serving God in a special way in the church!

Age-appropriate Incentives

Like other aspects of your ministry, incentives need to be age-appropriate in order to be effective. Here are some guidelines:

1. Early childhood incentives should be . . .

• *Readily achieved.* Small children will be discouraged quickly if they are too distant.

- *Given often.* Their attention span is too short to have a six-week incentive. A six-minute one is a lot more appropriate.

- *Non-competitive.* Early childhood is not a time for winning and losing; three-to-five-year-olds don't take losing very well. Don't believe me? Just try saying, "Everyone who can recite the Sunday School verse can have a cookie," and then try to manage all the crying of those who didn't get it done! You can have some receive more based on performance, but if you have a visible incentive, everyone needs to receive something.

2. Middle childhood incentives should be . . .

- *More individually focused.* You no longer need to have an incentive for everyone; kids in this age group can understand that you have to earn the incentive in order to get it.

- *More heart-focused.* Kids can now understand that their attitude—not just the behavior—has to be right.

- *More long-term.* You can expect them to respond to a distant incentive, such as "As soon as we can go six weeks with everyone staying in their chairs during the lesson time, our children's pastor has said he will stand on his head and sing 'Happy Birthday.'"

3. Tweens' and early adolescents' incentives should be . . .

- *Mostly team-focused.* Kids in this age group are often either reluctant to stand out or overeager to do so. Therefore, have the incentives follow this pattern: "If the whole group does _____, then we all get to _____." Encourage them to encourage each other!

- *Mostly heart-focused.* By now, the incentives should be all about attitudes and spiritual responses.

- *More about leadership.* As some of the other, more kid-friendly incentives wane in effectiveness, using your most mature kids in leadership roles needs to increase.

4. High school students' incentives should be . . .

- *More about discipleship.* That means a big focus on the heart; it's time to expect more intrinsic motivations from your teens who have had time to grow and develop in the Lord.

- *More about privileges and leadership.* It's time for your students to learn that there are blessings for following Christ (privileges and leadership) and consequences for not doing so.

Of course, in all of these areas, the incentives should not be in any way connected to how much a student is loved or accepted. In a ministry environment where every child or teen feels loved, an incentive can be an additional positive force to encourage faster spiritual growth, deeper Bible knowledge, greater service, and more godly responses. Try some incentives—you will find them to be great tools for your workers.

> Incentives should not be in any way connected to how much a student is loved or accepted.

Equip for War

Most ministry leaders think a lot about equipping their people for the work. The majority of the time, though, ministry doesn't fail because we don't equip well for work; it fails because we don't equip for war.

In a church Diane and I attended, I was an elder for a number of years. This church was a middle-sized congregation that had a very strong outreach to the community, and a particularly strong children's ministry. The Awana club was huge, using almost every room in the church. Vacation Bible School packed kids in as well; our Sunday morning services were growing, and God was blessing. We needed bigger facilities and made plans for construction.

In the midst of the growth, our new pastor preached a sermon about life after death—in particular, the resurrection of the saved and the unsaved. The message offended one of the deacons in the church, and the war started. Anyone who has been in ministry for a while has seen or heard about a war like this; these kinds of battles *destroy* ministry.

The debate was over a technicality about the resurrection, and it became ridiculous. However, neither party would back down. The deacon sent a letter to the denominational leadership, accusing our pastor of heresy. Needless to say, that didn't please the pastor, and he said the deacon needed to be disciplined.

We elders were caught in the middle. Over the space of about eight months, we had 50 elders' meetings to try to resolve this. I recognize, looking back, that we didn't always respond in the best possible way either, and the end result wasn't pretty. We did discipline the deacon, and he left, along with part of the congregation. The pastor left soon after that. Life had been sucked out of the church. We never did start construction on the new building, and ministries suffered. The church never recovered—never regained its previous vitality. The ministry *of* the church was defeated by the war *in* the church.

That is why it is so important that you equip for war; *that* is what will defeat your ministry. How do we equip for war? Ephesians 6:13-17 tells us:

> Therefore put on the full armor of God, so that when the day of evil comes, you may be able to stand your ground, and after you have done everything, to stand. Stand firm then, with the belt of truth buckled around your waist, with the breastplate of righteousness in place, and with your feet fitted with the readiness that comes from the gospel of peace. In addition to all this, take up the shield of faith, with which you can extinguish all the flaming ar-

rows of the evil one. Take the helmet of salvation and the sword of the Spirit, which is the word of God.

The context for this passage has to do with our spiritual struggle against Satan and his forces. That is *exactly* who our battle is against in ministry, but it manifests itself in the form of conflicts with other ministries, other workers and even other ministry leaders. Think about how the spiritual armor Paul describes can help you equip your workers for war:

The Belt of Truth

Two kinds of lies will destroy your ministry: the lie of false doctrines, and the lies that we tell about one another. I believe this passage is referring to the truth of God's Word, so that is the first application. Are you constantly encouraging your workers to know God's truth better and better? Are you helping them to deepen their understanding about God?

Truthfulness is also essential to ministry survival; lies, gossip, exaggerations or just the absence of true information can take down a ministry as well. Are you encouraging open, honest and truthful communication in your ministry? That is the second way you put on the belt of truth. Do you bristle at feedback that isn't complimentary, or do you encourage it? Do you refuse to allow gossip among your workers? Are you quick to deal with rumors before they spread? These may seem like difficult things to do, but trust me—your life will be more difficult if you do not do them.

The Breastplate of Righteousness

Living according to God's standards protects us in the war we are fighting. One disadvantage of being in ministry for a number of years (in my experience) is the grief of knowing fellow ministry leaders who have left this piece of the armor off. I've had to confront a Christian brother caught in adultery; I've served in leadership in a church where pride fueled a personal conflict so severe it split the church—in short, I have seen firsthand the devastation that comes to ministry work when a worker forgets to be equipped with his breastplate of personal holiness.

Don't just rely on your pastor's sermons to encourage godly living. *You* are the shepherd to your workers, so you do what you can as well to teach and exhort them to righteousness.

The Sandals of the Gospel of Peace

It's interesting to see how biblical scholars and pastors treat this phrase; some emphasize the word "gospel" and see this as a mandate for evangelism, while others emphasize "peace" and focus upon the cessation of hostilities between us and God that happens when we are saved. I prefer the latter, but I want to go one step further with the application. We ought to be equipped with the peace *of* God, now that we have peace *with* God. Our ministries ought to be characterized by peace among the workers. Instead, ministries are often battlegrounds for inflated egos, extra-biblical tradition and personal preference. As a leader, you are to equip your people with *peace*.

The Shield of Faith

"In addition to all this, take up the shield of faith, with which you can extinguish all the flaming arrows of the evil one" (Eph. 6:16). What are the fiery darts that Satan shoots at your workers? Most preachers talk about the darts of uncertainty, guilt or temptation. I agree. But I want to focus here on a different danger: trusting in *yourself* rather than putting faith in God.

I struggle with this way too often. I have lots of experience in working in ministry, and it is so easy to trust in my experience and giftedness. When I do, the ministry becomes about me rather than about God. I then get easily offended, or too egotistical, or too discouraged—all things that can take down a ministry.

I think I also do it right some times, when I trust in God for the results of my ministry like I should. Then I don't get so irritated if the schedule isn't followed. I don't get a big head if lots of people show up for a seminar or a deflated ego if they don't.

In whom or what are your workers trusting for spiritual fruit? Their giftedness? Their methods? Their experience? *Your* giftedness, methods or experience? Or God? When they keep their faith in God, it will protect them from a lot of harm.

The Helmet of Salvation

This is not the salvation of the past (i.e., receiving Christ as Savior), because that is already settled; Paul is writing to *believers* and he tells them to *put on* this armor. He is talking about the future, or final, aspect of salvation, when we finally participate in eternal life in heaven. In a parallel passage, Paul calls this part of the armor the *hope* of salvation (see 1 Thess. 5:8). Remember that *hope* in the Bible means "confidence."

So what's the point? Our *minds* are protected when we have an eternal perspective—when we are confident of heaven. This hope of salvation—the eternal perspective—is key to helping your workers deal with the frustrations of ministry.

Do you have an out-of-control toddler in your group? *If you can love this child and lead him toward Christ, putting up with him for an hour a week isn't bad.* An eternal perspective will help the workers have more patience.

Do you have an impossible work/ministry schedule that is wearing you out? *Sacrificing now becomes worth it when you know that what you do might affect eternity for someone else.* See—an eternal perspective will give you stamina.

This is an important focus for your workers—their *hope* of salvation for all eternity. When they are armed with that perspective, they will be protected from all sorts of satanic attack.

The Sword of the Spirit

How are you encouraging your workers to know God's Word themselves? Or are you just hoping that they are growing in their understanding when they attend worship services and small groups? Let me guess. You wish they knew Scripture better, but you are reluctant to push them too much or they might quit.

Remember to be a shepherd—lead them through your example. Let them know how you are diligently studying God's Word yourself to constantly improve your knowledge.

Then add some incentives. We're often reluctant to use incentives with our workers, but they *need* it. They're not doing it the way they should with merely intrinsic motivations, are they? Then they need (just like you and me) some extrinsic encouragement. Look back a few pages at the list of incentives. Think of some you might use to encourage your workers to grow in their knowledge of God's Word. The more they know, the more they should be able to wage an effective spiritual battle for the hearts and minds of your students.

Yes, you are leading people who are doing the work of the ministry. But you are also leading people who are under constant threat of attack. So put a tool in one of their hands and a weapon in the other. You don't want the work to get stopped because of the war.

Think and Talk About It

1. Think about your own experience. Have workers in the ministries you have been involved in suffered more from being under-equipped for the work of the ministry or for the war that threatens the ministry?

2. Think about the first ministry tool of a discipline system. How effective is the one in your ministry?

3. Are your workers clear about what to do and when to do it? Would you say your ministry structure could be improved by more flexibility or more rigidity?

4. Do you agree that loving is the most important skill that a worker should possess? Why or why not?

5. Do you have workers who could do a better job of showing love to their students? How could you begin to address that?

6. How many of your workers understand how to lead another person to Christ?

7. How might you use incentives to encourage your workers to do what you want them to do?

8. Would you better describe your ministry right now by the word "work" or by the word "war"? Why do you say that?

9. Which piece of the Christian's armor is most needed by your workers right now?

Note
1. Dr. Gregory C. Carlson, *Rock-Solid Teacher* (Ventura, CA: Gospel Light, 2006), p. 58

CONNECTIONS

*Then I said to the nobles, the officials and the rest of the people,
"The work is extensive and spread out, and we are widely separated
from each other along the wall. Wherever you hear the sound of the
trumpet, join us there. Our God will fight for us!" So we continued the
work with half the men holding spears, from the first light of dawn
till the stars came out. At that time I also said to the people, "Have every
man and his helper stay inside Jerusalem at night, so they can serve
us as guards by night and workmen by day."*
NEHEMIAH 4:19-22

Uzziel here again.

I didn't finish my story the last time we talked. I was concerned—no, more than that—I was really scared when I saw that Ammonite sword. Especially since I only had bricklayer's tools and didn't have a sword—or a shield—myself. But it wasn't long after those travelers gave us their report that here came Nehemiah's men with just what we needed; and in no time at all, we were equipped to fight if need be. You know, it's getting almost humorous: The minute I begin to worry about something, along comes Nehemiah or some of his men to deal with it. I want to tell you—he is really amazing. He said at the beginning that God had directed him here to help remove the disgrace from Jerusalem, and I believe it. I *really* believe it. How God is using him to help us do this wall-building is simply incredible.

Back to the weapons—between my brother Pediah and me, we got a full set of both armor and weapons. It helps that we are about the same size. So now, we take turns working on the wall and watching for the enemy. I must say, it is a great relief to feel equipped for whatever may come.

I do still have a concern, though. I was counting the workers on our section of the wall, and from what I can tell, there are fewer than a hundred of us. I don't know exactly how many soldiers the Ammonites can put together, but I am sure it is a lot more than that! Pediah asked those travelers that very question, and the man with the sword told him he believed it was upwards of 5,000 men. That means if they attack here, the odds are 50 to 1. And that's not in our favor. I also think it's pretty likely that they would attack our spot on the wall. We are so near to the road. Besides that, there are plenty of large rocks outside the walls for them to use for protection.

I can't help but feel vulnerable. I really do appreciate all that Nehemiah has done, and as I said, I believe his leadership is truly of God. But Pediah and I would surely feel a whole lot better if there was some way that the odds could be improved. We've talked about it, but we don't see how, with everyone working on the wall in different spots, it can be fixed.

"Uzziel! Come!"

Excuse me, Pediah is trying to get my attention . . .

You won't believe it. You won't believe it! I've been chuckling and shaking my head all the way back over here. Do you remember how I said that Nehemiah seems to have an answer for our concerns almost before we have them? Well . . . he did it again. Pediah was calling me over for a gathering of the workers. Nehemiah wanted to tell us about the system he has put into place. He's got a man with a trumpet with him, and he's going to use a trumpet blast as a signal to let us know if the enemy threatens to attack a certain place.

It's a great solution. The trumpet has a unique sound, and it really carries. I'm sure all us workers will be able to hear it. You don't know what a great relief it is to know that if the enemy does attack here, my friends and countrymen all have my back. To know we are supported . . .

Wow . . . I think we are going to be able to get this wall built after all!

The Importance of Connecting

Why do people stay in a ministry? While the results I've seen and heard are only anecdotal, the hands-down winner is . . . their sense of *connection*. A close connection with the ministry vision keeps them engaged and committed. So do their connections with those they are serving and, just as importantly, their connections with their co-workers.

> How faithfully people stay in a ministry is directly related to how connected they feel.

This motivation becomes a greater issue proportionately as the size of a church increases. In small churches, volunteers likely know one another from other aspects of church life. But in a very large church, the opposite is true; volunteers are *not* likely to know one another before they join a ministry. Therefore, the larger a church is, the more critical this issue becomes. I have served in large churches, medium-sized churches and small ones, so I have seen for myself how the issue of connection affects ministry.

Diane and I attended a small church, with fewer than 200 members, in Oxnard, California, when our kids were young. Some of our fellow workers in children's ministry were also in our adult Bible study; we sang with others in the choir, and had many opportunities to develop deep friendships. We were strongly connected to our ministry friends, and as a result there was a special vitality in our children's ministry. The next church we attended was a large one, with four services every week, in the San Fernando Valley. We rarely saw people we knew in the service we attended; we almost always sat next to total strangers. Our adult class on Sunday morning did not include any other volunteers from the ministries that we worked in, either. Nothing outside of our ministry involvement enhanced our relationships. We felt very unconnected, and before long, we went to another church. We left that church for one reason—we never got personally connected.

This issue is sort of a no-brainer, but we often overlook it. We know it is important, but we only *hope* it will happen, or we expect it to occur automatically. It comes down to the answer to this question:

Who would you rather serve beside—your best friend or a total stranger? "That's easy," you say. "My best friend." Now, we can't force our workers to be best friends with one another, but we can be intentional about nurturing and strengthening the sense of connection among team members.

How can we help our workers develop connections? To answer that, let's take another look at Nehemiah and the way he addressed this issue.

Nehemiah Saw It

Evidently Nehemiah's workers were not feeling very connected. His "trumpet signal system" was a practical way to make sure they would be able to support one another in the face of an attack by the enemy. But it is not the only way he created or restored connections. Look at how he has reconnected them throughout this story:

- They felt *dis*connected from their families, so Nehemiah *re*connected them—he posted them "by families" (Neh. 4:13).
- They were *dis*connected from the source of their strength, so Nehemiah *re*connected them—he told them, "Remember the Lord" (Neh. 4:14).
- They were *dis*connected from the benefit of a wall, so Nehemiah *re*connected them—he reminded them that it was for "your brothers, your sons and your daughters, your wives and your homes" (Neh. 4:14).

Now, the workers are feeling *disconnected from one another*. Nehemiah recognized this when he remarked, "We are widely separated from each other along the wall" (Neh. 4:19). Because he saw this, Nehemiah instituted the trumpet signal.

I remind you that they were all doing the same thing—*building the wall*—for the same purpose—*removing the disgrace*—and still they didn't feel connected. This can happen in our churches, too. Often, children's workers and youth workers are doing the same thing—*teaching young people*—for the same purpose—*that they would become devoted Christ followers*—and yet they never feel connected with one another.

The disconnection can happen because of a different time frame: If your church has multiple services, how do you help volunteers who are on different schedules feel like a team? Maybe it is about locations—more and more churches have two or more campuses, and their ministry leaders have a huge challenge. I appreciate the dilemma of Nina, a children's ministry director in Washington, DC, whose church I visited recently. Their church has five services and five locations, so she has to figure out how to overcome both location and time challenges.

It can happen because volunteers work with different age levels: How do you get children's workers to feel connected with youth workers? I've even heard people say, "I struggle just to get my Kindergarten teachers to feel connected with the First Grade teachers." For youth leaders, it is the challenge of encouraging Junior High workers to connect with High School workers.

Back to Nehemiah: The purpose of the trumpet was to enable the people to *connect* and *support* one another. In verse 20, Nehemiah says, "Wherever you hear the sound of the trumpet, *join us there*" (emphasis added). Why was this so important? To understand that, we first need to think about what disconnection does.

The Results of Disconnection

Disconnection Brings Fear

Certainly, the wall-workers were much more fearful because of the possibility that the enemy might attack their position, and they would have to defend it alone. There was no assurance of support. Would the other workers even know of an attack? Would they be able to get to the point of attack in time to help?

Your workers are probably not worried about Ammonites with fancy swords, but that doesn't necessarily mean they aren't afraid. Maybe they're nervous that a situation will arise that they don't know how to handle, and no one will be around to help them resolve it. Or maybe there's a child that's already giving them trouble, and they could use the wisdom of a more experienced volunteer, but they don't know anyone well enough to ask for advice.

On the other hand, connection reduces fear. When volunteers have confidence that they are not alone and that others have their backs, they are more willing to serve and more likely to stay.

Disconnection Produces Silos and Isolation

You've probably seen silos—those tall, usually blue buildings found on farms that are built to house grain after it has been harvested. Many of you have also probably heard the term applied to departments at your work that are disconnected from others and act too independently. In either case, "silos" just stand there, not connected to anything else, each doing its own thing. Businesses generally don't want silos, and church leaders shouldn't either. Yet, if you are a typical ministry leader in a local church, you are experiencing it right now. Maybe the "siloing" is happening for you by ministry: Sunday school teachers are not connected with Children's Church workers, or weekday club leaders are not connected with Sunday workers. Maybe there are cliques, or other disconnections between groups of people. Whatever the specifics, silos—the phenomenon of each ministry doing its own thing in isolation from the others—are not usually healthy.

In fact, we also create suspicion and sometimes even competition and jealousy by allowing disconnections to exist. Jennifer is a children's director in a large church. She confesses that she often feels resentful because the Junior High group always wants to use the gym—and gets to do it. Jennifer is a mom in her mid-30s, and she sees what the Junior High group does as "just a bunch of goofing off." Her Middle Elementary group would like to use the gym more often, but rarely gets it. She feels like she just gets the leftovers. She is not connected with the Junior High pastor's ministry direction, and because of the resentment she feels, she avoids building a relationship with him—and her frustration continues to grow.

Disconnection Inhibits Effectiveness

When we aren't connected, we are left to our own abilities, our own resourcefulness and our own understanding. Think about Paul's metaphor of the Church as a body. He asks, "If the whole body were an eye, where would the sense of hearing be?" (1 Cor. 12:17). Maybe one of your workers has 20/20 vision but can't hear so well. Or, more to the point, one worker may be great at teaching lessons but struggles to come up with ideas for fun activities that help kids apply principles in indirect ways. Another may come up with the best games ever, but could use some guidance about how best to discipline unruly students. When we are connected, we can feed off each other, complement one another's strengths and skills, and accomplish more for the kingdom of God!

Organizing for Mutual Support

As I mentioned before, it can be tempting to simply hope that connection will happen on its own. Unfortunately, that's not a very likely outcome. Some workers may reach out to others, but most will simply hunker down and do the best they can with what they have. As a leader, it's your responsibility to put structures in place that will foster a sense of connection and mutual support among your workers. Following are some suggestions for how you can lay effective groundwork for a genuinely connected ministry team:

Your Church as Jerusalem

Think of your church building as if it were the city of Jerusalem. On all sides, people are working on "rebuilding the wall": There's the nursery on the east side, teens on the west, middle elementary students on the north, and toddlers on the south. Got the picture?

If the enemy attacks the work on the nursery side (say, half of the workers don't show up), what happens? Are the nursery staffers left to figure it out for themselves? Who has their backs?

If there's a squabble between two of the boys in a Junior High small group, does the leader have anyone to supervise the rest while he deals with the two—or does he have someone else to handle the discipline problem? Who has his back?

I'm not suggesting you start a trumpet-blast signal system in your ministry. Although that would certainly draw attention . . . I *am* suggesting that you find ways for your workers to connect with and cover for one another. In fact, *plan* for coverage. (In the corporate world, they call it cross-training—the idea that one worker can be familiar enough with another's position to help out in a pinch.) You want your staff to feel like they are not simply a group of individuals serving, but an *army*. That is a challenge, I admit; but the more successful you are at getting them to feel that way, the more confident they will feel in their role and the more committed they will be to the work as a whole.

The Importance of Two

One basic way to establish connections within your ministry is to have volunteers work in pairs. This is a time-honored tradition; the Bible has several examples of ministry pairs:

- *Moses felt inadequate* for the task of leading the children of Israel out of Egypt, so God gave him Aaron for support (see Exod. 4:10-16).

- *Elijah was depressed.* He operated solo for a while; in fact, in 1 Kings 18 we read of his incredible victory on Mount Carmel over the false prophets. But what happened next? Queen Jezebel threatened his life, and Elijah ran, scared and despondent, into the desert. Part of his complaint to God was, "I am the only one left" (1 Kings 19:10,14). Discouraged, worn out and ready to just die, Elijah hit the bottom. God's directive to him in the following verses was pretty simple—"get back to work" (see v. 15) and "anoint Elisha to succeed you" (v. 16). From that point on, Elisha began to assist Elijah.

- *The disciples faced hardships.* When Jesus sent out the disciples in pairs to preach the gospel, He said, "I am sending you out like lambs among wolves" (Luke 10:3). In other words, "You are going to receive some pretty harsh treatment." Harsh treatment is difficult to endure if you are alone; it is much more bearable if you have a partner.

- *Paul traveled extensively.* On every missionary trip that the apostle Paul took, he had a companion—first, Barnabas, and later, Silas and Timothy. Likely, Paul did it partly to disciple, but it is evident that those men who traveled with him were a great encouragement and help to him as well.

Do your ministry volunteers feel they have a partner? I'm not talking about having someone to cover for them if they are absent (although that's important, as we discussed above). When I talk about a partner, I'm talking about someone who shoulders the ministry responsibility with them.

In our Awana training, we used to recommend that small-group ratios be one leader for every five children; now, we say two leaders for every ten children. Why? The ratio is the same, but the reality is different. We made the change partly because of child protection issues. But we also express it that way so that people immediately think about co-owning the responsibility for discipling a group of children.

The Importance of Team

I want to address a concern I have about children's ministries, and in particular, children's ministries in medium-sized or smaller churches.

Many of them operate like golf teams; I believe they need to function more like basketball teams. Know what I mean? Golf team members are on the same side, but how one performs has no impact on the performance of the others. If a golf team has a really weak performer, though, the whole team may go down to defeat because of it. A basketball team is different; their interaction is vital to their overall success.

Here's what I mean: In a typical Sunday School, the First Grade teacher is on her own. How well she does is not affected by the Kindergarten teacher or the Second Grade teacher. Each of the teachers, in fact, is totally responsible for his or her own ministry. I've already pointed out that this sort of isolation can lead to ineffectiveness and discouragement. It can also lead to the teacher staying beyond his or her calling because "there's no one else to do it."

I'm not advocating simply pulling all the classes together for the sake of the teachers, but I am advocating doing everything you can to work together as a team. Yes—combine the classes for an activity occasionally so teachers can work together or one teacher can have a break. Yes—have joint outings. Yes—pray together for each other.

To return to the basketball illustration for a moment: In basketball, players receive credit not only for the baskets they make themselves, but also for their efforts to assist other players in making baskets. We've talked about incentives before; in addition to rewarding volunteers for things they do well in their own roles, think about ways you can encourage workers to help their colaborers toward success.

Mutual Support Events

In addition to providing mutual support through ministry structures, you can also do it through events—both large-scale gatherings and day-to-day points of interaction. Here's a question for you: *What is your "trumpet"?* What events do you use to call your workers together and enable them to meet one another's work and warfare needs? Here are some suggestions:

A Rallying Point

Have a certain location in your church where all workers must go at least once each time they volunteer. If it is mandatory for the purpose of child protection—signing in and out, picking up nametags, and so forth—you will see it become a regular visiting place for them. Add some refreshments, and suddenly you have a teachers' lounge—a spot where your workers will begin to connect with one another over time. Be intentional about making it a place in which they would *like* to linger.

Chuck Swindoll recommends having a rallying point, and then he adds:

> A rally point is a *place*, but it also suggests a *principle*. The trumpet would establish the place. Nehemiah ordered, "Whenever you hear that trumpet sound, run to the spot where the bugler stands." The purpose of the rally point is to ensure that people face their attackers together. The

principle: don't try to fight alone. To overcome discouragement, always face adversity together.[1]

A Quick Connection

Have brief meetings—5 to 10 minutes long—before or right after your workers serve. If you do it before, take attendance—there has to be some accountability for them to be there on time. If you do it after, announce it right before the end of the ministry time. Regular connections, even for a few minutes, can accomplish a lot if you plan carefully.

You can accomplish a lot of what I have recommended in this book in these brief meetings:

- You can pray for your workers to encourage them.
- You can use this time to reinforce what you want them to focus on.
- You can find out how you can better equip them by asking questions such as, "What is frustrating you?" or "What can I do to make your ministry easier for you?"

A Social Network

Facebook pages or Twitter (or whatever else is created after this book is published) provide a less personal—but still valuable—way of connecting volunteers with one another. Facebook, which can include photos, is especially helpful in large churches where it is a bigger challenge for workers to get to know one another.

Regular Training and Prayer Sessions

We've talked about the importance of both training and prayer before. The beauty of these sessions is that they can serve not only to equip volunteers for the work and refocus them on God, but also to give workers opportunities to get to know one another better and bond as a team. Sharing their ideas and concerns about ministry, participating in recreational activities, learning new skills together—all of these activities can foster deeper connections among those who are serving in your program.

A couple of things to keep in mind: Schedule these sessions well ahead of time, and let prospective workers know when you recruit them that you will expect their attendance. That's a critical issue—to avoid misunderstandings and potential attitude issues down the road, you need to say something like this:

> Stephanie, we'd love to have you work with the seventh-graders if you can fulfill the commitments. This is a critical time in kids' lives, and we need workers to be equipped to really be effective in ministering to them. What this ministry position requires is a couple of hours of preparation each week, attendance at our training events each quarter, and of course being there each Sunday at 9 A.M. The training events are critical to everyone being able to serve well, so we expect all of our volunteers to attend. Now, if that scares you, I want you to know we are here to equip you and help you and stand behind you.

Getting People to Come

I expect that everyone reading this book has agreed with the premise of this chapter so far. I also believe that you are thinking, *Yes—it's good to do this, but how do I get them to come?* I hear this concern from ministry leaders more often than just about anything else. So—here are my top 10 ways to get people to come to training and prayer meetings:

10. Have People They Like to Be Around There as Well

Of course, people are more likely to attend if they are friends with the others that come. If they are not, then building friendships ought to be a primary agenda item until their fellow workers become people they like to be around.

9. Inspire Them

Your workers need vision and direction. Talk about your spiritual goals in a positive, exciting way. Use a brief Bible study, or testimonies from their students, or a set of goals, or statistics, or charts of progress. You may want to invite a special speaker for this. You could also inspire participants by asking students to come and share what their teachers mean to them!

8. Recognize Them

Show personal appreciation; give out awards or recognition for anything you can think of, and commend them for little things that they do. Have a "Teacher of the Month." Recognize "Most Likely to Be on Time," "Best Greeter," "Most Effective Lesson," "The Biggest Heart"—anything that will help your people to feel appreciated. Get the students to secretly write notes of appreciation to your workers and read them out loud.

One year in my ministry as an Awana missionary, I had some communication that I really wanted every church to hear, and I needed a new tactic to get each congregation to be represented at my meeting. So I decided to give out surprise appreciation awards to a key person from each church. I sent the publicity materials to that person but didn't say anything about the appreciation award. Then I called another one of their workers on the phone and told him or her, "I have this meeting coming up, and I sent the information to Joe. But what Joe doesn't know is that we are going to give him a surprise award. Will you find out if he is planning to come? If for some reason he is not, then tell him, 'You may want to go, because Larry was planning on giving you an award.'" It was amazing how many who weren't planning on coming changed their minds when they heard they were getting an award. We ended up with great attendance. Just one caution if you are prompted to try something like this: You can really only do this once. It won't have the same effect a second time.

7. Don't Bore Them

Want to kill attendance in future meetings? Then simply go over things that could be delivered by text, email or in a flyer. Or take a long time to share details. If you want your people to come back, you need to make sure there is a compelling reason for them to be there—information that could not be received, or received as well, another way. Keep things moving—a good rule is that you must do something different every 20 minutes. That isn't always possible, but you can at least change the method of presentation.

6. Give Them Something
Always keep your eyes open for free stuff that you can give your workers; ask businesses to donate gift cards or coupons—whatever you can find. Use them as a means to express your appreciation.

5. Involve Them
If you always lead the meeting and control the agenda, people may feel their attendance is unnecessary. So—involve as many as possible. Ask someone ahead of time to lead the prayer time: "Mary, our prayer time can be better than it has been. Could you lead it at this next meeting and make it more effective?" Mary will be at the next meeting, because she feels responsible for part of the meeting. Have one person share about a spiritual victory in your ministry, ask another to talk about a challenge—whatever you do, involve others in the meeting. Yes, it takes more time to plan for the meeting this way, but trust me, you *will* reap the benefits.

Remember that in the last chapter I encouraged you to develop the skill of listening? This is a perfect chance to practice it. If you give people an opportunity to speak—even if it is in table groups—they will appreciate it. Kris Reed from Kansas says, "Starting the meeting with praise and prayer needs also lets each person feel like they are being heard."

4. Make Them Laugh
People need to have fun! When a training or planning meeting is over, you might evaluate it by asking, "Did they laugh at some point in this meeting?" Humor is not my strong suit, but I believe that any good meeting will have some in it. So how do you do it? Play a game. Tell a funny story. Create a humorous "Find the Mistake" video or slide show to help workers align with standard procedures or policies. Impromptu skits often work well.

My favorite game still is Family Feud. It's so easy to incorporate learning in a humorous or fun way with the "We surveyed one hundred people . . ." approach. You can make it "We surveyed one hundred kids" (and relax, you can *pretend* you surveyed them)—it's just a fun way to make sure your people have the information they need to do their jobs effectively.

3. Solve Their Problems

Stay in touch with what frustrates your people. Then propose solutions as part of your training. Your meetings should be a place where they find answers to what frustrates *them*, not just where they hear about what frustrates *you*.

What do you do if they aren't frustrated? Take Crystal—she is a very competent fourth-grade teacher. She loves her kids, and they, being the age they are, not only love her back, but also express their affection to her. Crystal is content and fulfilled—why does she need problem solving when she has no problems? Believe it or not, you've got to create some problems for Crystal. No, not by giving her some uncontrollable kids. You do it by expanding her vision for her ministry. How can she reach more children? How can she retain them better? How can parents be more involved? Ministry should always have some tension in it that workers feel. When workers are content, it means that their vision isn't big enough. As people called to fulfill the Great Commission, we should all feel some "holy discontent" while there is still disciple-making work to be done in the world.

One of the most effective (and popular) workshops we offer in our Awana training conferences is entitled "Why Tanner Never Came Back." It encourages people to think for a moment about the kids they *lost* rather than the kids they *have*. That kind of discontent is critical for workers like Crystal who are too comfortable in their roles.

2. Invite Them to Your Home

People like to go to a home for a meeting, not a church. It's also amazing how your workers will feel a little more obligated to show up when the gathering is held at someone's home. Jane Larson, from Iowa, says, "They love to see each other's homes, and there is a sense of fellowship that takes place. It also increases ownership among the lay staff."

1. Feed Them!

Without question, this one is the most common answer when you ask ministry leaders, "How do you get your volunteers to show up?" Of course, I'm not talking about a stale cookie after a two-hour meeting; I mean a barbecue, potluck, dessert or something like that.

Nehemiah used a trumpet. I've told you some of the things I do. Now it's your turn. Find an approach that works to connect your people with one another, and then use it! Remember that, however you accomplish it, people who feel connected with the purpose of your ministry, with you, and with their co-workers are much less likely to walk away!

Think and Talk About It

1. Take the perspective of a wall worker in Nehemiah's crew. Why was the trumpet such a good idea?

2. What connects you to your ministry? In other words, what is the primary reason you keep at it? Do you know what others around you would say?

3. On a scale of 1 to 10, how connected with one another do you feel your workers are? What do you observe that makes you assign that rating?

4. How connected is your ministry with others in the church? How do you evaluate the effects of that level of connection?

5. Which support events have you found to be the most effective? Do you need a fresh approach to meetings?

6. Look through the ideas about how to get workers to come to meetings. Is there one or more you would like to try?

Note
1. Charles Swindoll, *Hand Me Another Brick* (Nashville, TN: W Publishing Group, 2006), p. 62.

EXAMPLE

*So we continued the work with half the men holding spears, from the
first light of dawn till the stars came out. At that time I also said to the
people, "Have every man and his helper stay inside Jerusalem at night,
so they can serve us as guards by night and workmen by day."
Neither I nor my brothers nor my men nor the guards with me took
off our clothes; each had his weapon, even when he went for water.*
NEHEMIAH 4:21-23

This is Uzziel again. I believe this will be my last report. This
has been the most incredible, most amazing experience! I
want you to notice where I am—standing on the wall. Do
you see that? I'm on the wall! Yes, it is done—finished! And
we did it in 52 days. Did you get that? *Fifty-two* days! I can't
tell you how, with all the challenges we faced, but it is complete, and it looks really, really fine!

I've learned so much through this process . . . about me,
about Nehemiah, but mostly about God and my relationship
with Him.

As I reflect back over this whole wall-building project, I
think I was most impressed with Nehemiah's style of leadership. It was . . . so . . . different . . . so . . . humble. Every king or
royal person I had ever seen treated others like dirt, so when
I first heard that Nehemiah came from the royal palace in
Susa, I fully expected him to be the same.

Were my expectations wrong! As we were getting close
to the end of building the wall, Nehemiah came by to encourage us, and he stunk—literally! In fact, I thought at the

time, "He smells like one of the workers!" That may not seem to be a big thing to you, but it was to us. Royalty and all those ruler-types usually put that perfumy stuff on themselves, and they avoid getting sweaty at all costs. That's why it seemed so strange that Nehemiah was smelly. Then—I thought about it. Nehemiah had been working long hours—as long as, if not longer than, anyone else. One of his servants said that Nehemiah just slept in his clothes, because he was working from dawn until well after dark.

I don't know how familiar you are with my culture, but we are not used to leaders acting like that. Kings stay in their palaces and send out soldiers to fight—even die—for their greedy egos. Fathers abuse their kids. Landowners often treat their servants brutally as they make them do all the hard and dirty work.

To have a leader who worked hard right alongside of us was certainly strange, but, wow, was it motivating! I think . . . no, I know: The single biggest reason that we finished the wall so quickly was Nehemiah's example. While we saw many wise things that he did and said, his humble, selfless spirit was absolutely the most influential.

I don't know about you, but I want to be a leader like that. I will probably never be a governor or an official, and I may never even be an elder at the gate, but I can be that kind of a dad. I can be that kind of influence on my younger relatives and on my neighbors. I want to be that kind of businessman, too. As I return to goldsmithing now, I've been thinking about how I could treat my customers the same way that Nehemiah treated all of us.

Maybe I can . . . and if I can, may God get the glory!

I suspect that every one of you who reads this book has heard before that you must be an example. I'm sure that 99 percent of you have *said* that to others as well. Yet, I know from personal experience that

Example 157

while being an example is easy to talk about, it is much harder to actually do it. You know that too, don't you?

I am sure you also recognize that this is the one thing we must not miss. While you can still be effective as a leader without emphasizing families ministering together or equipping workers thoroughly, if you are not an example to your ministry volunteers, you will fail. That is why it is fitting that this is the final, climactic chapter of the book.

You *have* to be an example. My good friend Mike Broyles is a ministry veteran. He's served in small churches and large churches, and he has mentored dozens of younger ministry leaders. He says, "The primary way we teach—no, the *only* way we teach—is by example." I couldn't agree more.

You will destroy your effectiveness without it. You will hinder the Kingdom. You will be a disgrace.

"I Am an Example"

Nehemiah was the author of this book that bears his name, though Ezra may have been the scribe. It is unique among the books of Scripture because the narratives in it are all written in the first person. In fact, it is essentially the memoirs of Nehemiah. I am intrigued that he carefully points out, in several instances, how he is an example to the people. Why did he draw attention to his example? Was he bragging?

The idea of *being* an example intimidates me enough. But I am really reluctant to *say* I am one. (When I said earlier that it's easy to talk about being an example, I didn't mean this kind of talking about it.) Do you feel the same way? We all understand that ministry leadership requires modeling. Yet, we usually want others to recognize our example rather than to point it out ourselves. That is why I've marveled at the apostle Paul. He told the Corinthians, "I urge you to imitate me" (1 Cor. 4:16) and instructed the Philippians, "Join with others in following my example, brothers" (Phil. 3:17). I've wondered, *Could I say that to those around me? Would I feel comfortable saying to them, "Follow my example"?*

In preparing to write this book, I have asked many ministry friends to contribute their thoughts. For this chapter, I asked them, "How are you an example to your workers?" Their answers have been uncommonly similar—everyone has responded with something like, "That's really hard to say . . ." and each one has been a little reluctant to tell me specifics. I think they are intimidated as well. Why is it so hard to say, "I am an example"?

- *Because we want to be humble.* Of course, I want to *be* an example; I just am reluctant to *say* I am because others may interpret it as being boastful. And if they interpret it that way, I would end up being a bad example, not a good one.

- *Because we know ourselves.* There are so many ways that I am not a good example to others. I can think of lots of ways that I don't measure up. Do I *really* qualify as an example? I'd rather wait to broadcast it until I have my act together a little better.

- *Because others know our faults as well.* My co-workers, my wife, my kids—they all know a bunch of my spiritual blemishes. If I say, "Follow my example," will they be thinking of my weaknesses and failures?

It's hard to say, but we've got to say it. Then we have to live up to our words if we want to motivate others. So . . . you say it. Say quietly to yourself right now, *I am an example.* Go ahead; say it. You can say it out loud if you want to do so.

Now, let's learn from Nehemiah how to be one.

Nehemiah's Example

It's accurate to say here, I believe, that all of the previous chapters have revealed how Nehemiah was an example:

- He prayed as a first response.
- He cared about family relationships.

Example   159

- He kept his focus on God.
- He made the task personally meaningful to the workers.
- He was careful to equip them well.
- He provided connections for the workers.

You know those mirrors in clothing stores in which you can see yourself from several angles? I like to think of this book as something like one of those—we've taken a look at Nehemiah from a number of different directions, and he's come out looking pretty good. You could say that he was exemplary in many ways. However, in this chapter, I want to unpack three views—three specific ways that he models leadership for us. Here they are: Nehemiah was an example through his (1) sad face, (2) plain food, and (3) dirty clothes.

Nehemiah's Sad Face

The king asked me, "Why does your face look so sad when you are not ill?" (Neh. 2:2).

I'm a "crier." I inherited it from my dad, I think. Even though he had a pretty tough life as a cattle rancher, he had a tender heart. Little things made him choke up. Spiritual things made him cry. Patriotic things made the tears come, just because he was wired that way. When I was young, I was embarrassed because he was emotional, and embarrassed because I was, too. I knew others thought that real men didn't cry.

Now I see it differently. It is still hard for me to hide my tears, even when I'm teaching a large group, but consistent comments from my audiences have helped me understand that as long as I am not manufacturing false emotion, it is one of my best strengths in influencing others. I'm not afraid to reveal my feelings to those who serve with me and under me when something moves me.

I think Nehemiah was the same way. Think about it: He was *cupbearer* to the king, but he couldn't hide his true feelings (see Neh. 2:1). How significant was that? A little background will help:

A cupbearer was "an officer of high rank at ancient courts, whose duty it was to serve the wine at the king's table. On account of the constant fear of plots and intrigues, a person must be regarded as thoroughly trustworthy to hold this position. He must guard against poison in the king's cup, and was sometimes required to swallow some of the wine before serving it. His confidential relations with the king often endeared him to his sovereign and also gave him a position of great influence."[1]

Archaeologists have discovered a list of salaries paid to the highest Assyrian officials. This record reflects the general values of similar posts in the Persian administration. After the commanding general, the prime minister and the palace authority came the cupbearer, who earned the fourth-largest salary in the kingdom.[2]

So Nehemiah was well paid, highly regarded and influential. Even so, he was a servant of the king, and the last thing you wanted to do as a servant of the king was look sad, because:

It was against Persian law for a servant ever to show sadness in the king's presence. In fact, Nehemiah knew that he was in danger of being severely punished for demonstrating anything but a joyful countenance while on duty. He could have been demoted—or even imprisoned.[3]

But Nehemiah, apparently, couldn't help it. King Artaxerxes, when he received the wine from his cupbearer, said, "Why does your face look so sad when you are not ill? This can be nothing but sadness of heart" (Neh. 2:2). With so much at risk, why *did* Nehemiah's face look sad? I believe it was because he just couldn't help being transparent. He was wired that way. We continue to see this throughout Nehemiah's book. He's pretty transparent in what he recorded—often revealing his thoughts and motives. For instance, it interests me that he said in Nehemiah 2:2, "I was very

Example   161

much afraid." That's not usually what political leaders in his day wrote in their memoirs—but Nehemiah did. He wasn't afraid to bare his heart.

What Letting Others See Your Heart Means

People want to know you are "real." That means they want to understand those thoughts and feelings that you are tempted to keep locked up inside where no one can get to them. Transparency is a valued quality in today's culture, especially with younger generations. If your workers think you are *not* this way, they will be more reluctant to follow your lead. More specifically, here's what letting others see your heart means to me:

Being Willing to Reveal Your Failures and Vulnerabilities

Everyone has them, and we know they help us grow—and yet our instinct is still to try very hard to hide our weaknesses. The thing is, when we put up those perfect fronts, we miss opportunities to encourage those around us—who also have failures and vulnerabilities in their lives. Though it's difficult to do, being honest about our mistakes is a great way to lead, because when people see *that you don't hide your failures, they will have hope that God can use them as well.*

I was visiting my son's church one time, and the pastor told a story about a visitor they had had several years before. He was emphasizing how he wanted their church to be a place where anyone could come to find Christ. He related how a woman came to visit, but stayed outside the church. One of the pastors asked her if he could help. She said, "I would like to go to church, but I don't know if I'm allowed to." When the associate pastor asked why she thought that, she replied, "Because I'm a topless dancer."

Without hesitation, the pastor said, "Of course you can—you can come sit right up front in the first row with all of the other sinners and cheats and thieves—and that's just the pastors!" The preacher related that because of that response, the woman came inside. She has since been saved, left her "profession," and has now started a ministry to other dancers.

I think it was the one phrase—"and that's just the pastors!"—that did it. With those transparent, unexpected words, this church leader disarmed a woman burdened by her own failures, made her feel accepted, and therefore opened the door for her to find Christ.

Letting People See Your Grief
Like failure, grief is often something we try to keep to ourselves. Maybe we're afraid people will think we're weak—or that we don't have enough faith—if we let them see our sorrow and tears. By hiding your grief, though, you may be depriving a fellow believer of a blessing that they would receive through comforting and encouraging you. In addition, *when people see your transparency, they will also risk sharing their hurts with you.*

Letting People See Your Uncertainties
When people are invited into your decision-making processes, they will be honored that you are including them as "advisors." They become encouraged and will begin to share your vision. It's not important that you know *everything* as a leader. It is pretty important that you have a clear picture of where you are going, but the more your workers can contribute to how you are going to get there, the more whole-heartedly they will own the process. Once more, when people see that you are comfortable not having all the answers and learning as you go, they may become more willing to share ideas and insights that they have been formulating.

The Reasons Behind Nehemiah's Sad Face
Why we are transparent in our feelings is also important. If it is because we are emotionally fragile, people will tire of it. If we are insincere, or seem to others to try to manipulate through it, people will be angered by it. The reasons behind Nehemiah's sad face are critical to understand. Here are some of the things that contributed to his somber countenance:

He Was Passionate to Protect God's Reputation
We're not told how the people in Jerusalem viewed the broken-down wall, but we know how Nehemiah interpreted it: He saw it

Example   163

as a *disgrace* to the reputation of God. He was so overwhelmed by this thought that he couldn't keep it from showing on his face.

I can be motivated to be an example so that people think well of me, or I can be an example so that people think well of God. I confess that too often I am motivated to be an example so that *my* reputation is preserved.

Many people in America don't think much of Christian leaders. The broadly publicized moral failures of several of our high-profile pastors and leaders have left a huge stench, and God is paying the price. "*Is* Jesus the only way?" people ask. "If He's so great, why does it appear that believing in Him makes no difference in people's behavior?" In fact, many see Christians as *less* moral, *more* judgmental, and therefore more hypocritical than non-Christians. The grievous result is that God's reputation is tarnished in their eyes.

Many adherents of other religions—Islam, for example—view Christianity through the lens of moral behavior, and we fail miserably. While I have never lived in a Muslim country, I have friends who have. One of those friends is Chris, who spent time working in Saudi Arabia on rocket engines that propelled oil through the pipelines. He has related how surprised his Islamic co-workers were to learn that he didn't cheat on his wife or indulge in other vices—because that is what they thought Christians did (they had been primarily influenced by what they saw on television). Is it any wonder that so many Muslims are opposed to Christianity influencing their culture and want to keep it out?

As a Christian leader, I must be most concerned about what people will think of God. I believe it is significant that Nehemiah did not say, when speaking before the people of Jerusalem, "Let us rebuild the wall so *we* are no longer disgraced." Instead, his concerns—and his words—were directed toward removing the disgrace from God's reputation. At the conclusion of the wall building, people's view of God had indeed changed: "All the surrounding nations . . . realized that this work had been done with the help of our God" (Neh. 6:16).

Nehemiah was following the example of Moses. When the children of Israel rebelled because of the report of the 10 spies whom Moses had sent to search out Canaan, God threatened to destroy them and start over with Moses: "I will strike them down with a plague and destroy them, but I will make you into a nation greater and stronger than they" (Num. 14:12). That had to have been quite a temptation for Moses. He too was frustrated with the people, and God was offering him the promise that had been made generations earlier to Abraham, Isaac and Jacob. But Moses' response demonstrates that he was entirely focused on what this would do for God's reputation:

> Then the Egyptians will hear about it . . . They will tell the inhabitants of this land about it . . . If you put these people to death all at one time, the nations who have heard this report about you will say, "The LORD was not able to bring these people into the land he promised them on oath" (Num. 14:13-16).

Moses' concern was about what others would think of God. In the New Testament, Jesus told us, in His sermon on the mount, to have the same kind of focus. He said, "Let your light shine before men, that they may see your good deeds and praise your Father in heaven" (Matt. 5:16). What startles me about this verse is the word "they." It refers to "men"—that is, all humanity, even pagans—and *they* are the ones who "praise your Father in heaven." Think about the exhortation: our "light," or testimony, is to be such that even pagans praise God. That is an incredibly high standard—but it also illustrates the target we are talking about here: We are to protect *God's* reputation.

God's reputation is under scrutiny by the cultural eyes of a watching world. We must have a passion to protect it.

Example   165

Is that what motivates you? Would it concern you so deeply that you couldn't keep your face from revealing your heart?

He Understood His Culture

In the chapter on motivating through a focus (and earlier in this one, too), I talked about the fact that Nehemiah's passion—what would have made him pound the podium—was not the *broken-down wall*, but the *spiritual disgrace*. The Scripture text made that point clearly, but I was still puzzled by the question, Why was a broken-down wall such a big disgrace? From my twenty-first-century American viewpoint, I didn't get it—because I use a different cultural lens than Nehemiah did. Let me share a little bit of what I have learned about city walls in his day.

First, speaking generally, strong walls were cultural symbols of power and excellence. It's hard for us to comprehend, because our cities don't have walls. In fact, we wouldn't even dream of having walls around them, would we? But in Nehemiah's time, when wars were fought at close range, walls were critical for the protection of a city. A good wall provided a great defense against foot soldiers, cavalry and charioteers. In Old Testament times, the walls were a status symbol that spoke not only to the strength of a people group, but also to the perception of that people's God. As Raymond Brown states:

> Far more serious than the physical desolation is the spiritual *disgrace*. It is a reproach to the name of God, a matter for scorn and abuse among Jerusalem's pagan neighbours and visitors. The sight of those collapsed walls for well over a century has created the impression in the pagan mind that Israel's God has abandoned his rebellious people and is no longer on their side.[4]

Second, Jerusalem's broken-down wall in particular was a reminder of terrible humiliation. The destruction of the city, recorded in 2 Kings 25, was the lowest point of the darkest days in Israel's history. Continual sinning by the Israelites had prompted

God's judgment, which was carried out by Nebuchadnezzar, the king of Babylon. For decades, the greatest pride of Israel—Jerusalem and its temple—were left in ruins.

Drive past a church in America that has an unkempt lawn, and what do you think? Here's what I think, because I am a product of middle-class American culture: "That church is tired and visionless, and probably not much spiritual is happening there." In my mind, the reputation of that church is tarnished because I see the weedy overgrown lawn. But my thoughts go beyond that: I'm actually a little embarrassed to have that church property represent my faith to its community. Now, there is nothing biblical about having a well-manicured lawn; this is purely a cultural thing. Yet, in our American thinking, an unkempt lawn can tarnish God's reputation.

Everyone views ministry methods through their own cultural lenses. I learned that on one of my first trips to Russia: In the more traditional churches there, when a pastor preaches, he is expected to be somber, respectful and reverent. Therefore, there is no excessive smiling if you are the preacher, and it is really a no-no to tell jokes. One of my traveling companions, a pastor, was invited to preach in a church we visited. Not knowing the congregation's expectations, he began his sermon with what was probably his usual custom—telling a joke. I realized what he was doing, but I couldn't stop him. The translator seemed to know what was coming, too, and looked panicky. Fortunately (I guess), the joke was a word play that didn't translate, so the people didn't know it was supposed to be funny. When no one laughed, the *pastor* didn't know what to do—and there was an awkward pause for a few seconds. But the fact that the joke didn't translate probably saved his American hide that day.

The specifics vary depending on the time and place, but the principle is the same: We need to be familiar enough with the culture in which we are living and ministering to recognize the aspects of our lives, churches and ministries that damage God's reputation in the eyes of those around us. Consider your own situation. Do you have broken-down walls that are a cultural disgrace? Maybe your ministry "walls" have been ruined because of

Example   167

an enemy attack, or maybe they have eroded because of other things—like neglect, lost purpose, apathy, lack of focus, or too tight of a grip on tradition. Do you have a passion to be culturally excellent? Why? Is it so you can protect God's reputation—or your own?

What shows on your face? What would people say drives you?

Trust me. If you abandon protecting your own interests in favor of protecting God's, people will respond. They will follow. And they will stay faithful in working at your side.

Nehemiah's Plain Food

Moreover, from the twentieth year of King Artaxerxes, when I was appointed to be their governor in the land of Judah, until his thirty-second year—twelve years—neither I nor my brothers ate the food allotted to the governor. But the earlier governors—those preceding me—placed a heavy burden on the people and took forty shekels of silver from them in addition to food and wine. Their assistants also lorded it over the people. But out of reverence for God I did not act like that. Instead, I devoted myself to the work on this wall. All my men were assembled there for the work; we did not acquire any land.

Furthermore, a hundred and fifty Jews and officials ate at my table, as well as those who came to us from the surrounding nations. Each day one ox, six choice sheep and some poultry were prepared for me, and every ten days an abundant supply of wine of all kinds. In spite of all this, I never demanded the food allotted to the governor, because the demands were heavy on these people (Neh. 5:14-18).

Nehemiah didn't take advantage of his privileged position; in fact, he chose to do the opposite. He ate plain food because that is all the people had to eat.

One of my best friends and co-workers in ministry is Richard Yandle. He is in a very respected position as the Executive Director of U.S. Missions for Awana. His responsibilities include overseeing more than 200 missionaries and more than 2,000 high-level volunteers. Whenever we host guests in our facilities (which we do often) and he is involved, you can count on one thing happening during the meals: *Richard will bus the tables.* Sometimes, those who are organizationally under him are a little embarrassed to have him clear their tables. But he does it because he simply loves to serve. Needless to say, his humility also motivates people to appreciate him and serve with him.

That is the kind of thing Nehemiah did: It would have been *culturally acceptable* for him to eat special food, but he didn't. It would have been *culturally acceptable* for him to direct the building of the wall from a protected location, but he didn't.

I appreciate Richard very much—perhaps more so because I've seen the opposite in ministry as well. I remember once using a church facility for a conference on a Saturday. It was in southern California in the fall, when the weather is ideal, and we planned to set up some displays outside the entrance, in and near the parking lot. The pastor's secretary warned us, "Don't set up anything in the senior pastor's parking spot. He generally doesn't come in on Saturday, but his space is to be always reserved for him." So we didn't. But we *did* set up some tables in the parking space next to his. And wouldn't you know it—he came in that morning. When he saw the tables close to his parking spot, he was upset, and he let us know that if we wanted to use his church again, we'd better not repeat that mistake. He was afraid his car door might get scratched. That only confirmed what I saw in him—he felt entitled to special privileges because he was the senior pastor. Maybe he was entitled—I won't judge that—but his actions certainly *did not* make me a fan of his.

In Philippians, Paul tells us to follow Jesus' example in being this kind of person:

> Your attitude should be the same as that of Christ Jesus: Who, being in very nature God, did not consider equality with God something to be grasped, but made himself nothing, taking the very nature of a servant (Phil. 2:5-7).

Example   169

If you have read this book this far, you are no doubt a ministry leader, and you probably have a few perks in your position. Let me encourage you to be a model by *not* taking extra advantage of your position. Give up your entitlement once in a while—and be like Jesus! Here is an A to Z list of ways you can "in humility consider others better than [yourself]" (Phil. 2:3):

- **A**ccept criticism without responding in return
- **B**less a little child
- **C**lean a whiteboard
- **D**rop a handwritten note of appreciation in the mail
- **E**mpty the trash can yourself
- **F**eed people some food
- **G**ive someone a cup of cold water
- **H**andle a problem right away
- **I**ntroduce someone and say something really nice about him or her
- **J**ot a thank you to your senior pastor
- **K**ill a rumor
- **L**eave a tip for those who clean the church restrooms
- **M**ake a phone call to say thanks
- **N**otice someone else's kindness
- **O**pen the door for someone when they don't expect it
- **P**ick up some clutter
- **Q**uote someone in your message (in a way that honors them)
- **R**emember someone's name after hearing it just one time
- **S**tack some chairs
- **T**ake somebody a cup of coffee
- **U**ntangle some extension cords
- **V**olunteer for the dirtiest job
- **W**ash somebody's feet
- "**X**press" thanks unexpectedly
- **Y**ield to a request from your senior pastor without complaining
- **Z**ip your lip

Nehemiah's Dirty Clothes

Neither I nor my brothers nor my men nor the guards
with me took off our clothes; each had his weapon, even
when he went for water (Neh. 4:23).

There was no privileged class with Nehemiah; he imposed the
same standard upon himself and his inner circle of leadership that
was upon all the workers. He must have insisted to his brothers
and his other assistants that they work as hard as everyone else.
That was a pretty high standard: Verse 21 says that they "worked
from the first light of dawn till the stars came out."

When I was a young youth pastor in southern California, one
of my students, Kumi, invited one of his baseball friends to attend
some of our activities. Kumi played on his high school's baseball
team, and he had recently trusted Christ as his Savior. In fact, he
was the first student to become a Christ-follower under my ministry. Though God has led our lives in different directions, we have
stayed in touch and remain good friends even today.

Alvin, the baseball teammate that Kumi invited, was already a
believer and attended another church that didn't have a youth
group. Because of that, Alvin became a part of our group, too, and
it was the start of a life-long friendship for me with two special
young men.

Kumi was a good baseball player, but Alvin was *very* good—in-
credibly good. He received a full baseball scholarship to Arizona
State University and became an All-American. Later, Alvin Davis
was drafted by the Seattle Mariners and began a significant profes-
sional career in 1984. In fact, that first year, he was American
League Rookie of the Year and was selected for the American
League All-Star team. He enjoyed eight productive years with the
Mariners and certainly was paid accordingly.

But when I think of Alvin in that period of his life, I don't picture him in a baseball uniform; instead, I remember him with a
broom in his hand.

Why? During the off-season, Alvin lived in southern California and attended my mother- and father-in-law's small church. At

Example   171

the time, they were meeting in temporary facilities—renting a YWCA meeting hall that many other groups also used. Every Sunday morning, my father-in-law would be responsible for unlocking the facility, getting it cleaned up from all those other groups, and preparing it for the worship service. He would sweep the floor, set up folding chairs, and perform other janitorial duties.

When we would visit, I can remember going with my father-in-law to get the building opened up and finding Alvin—the American League All-Star and Rookie of the Year—ready to help. Alvin would sweep the floor, set up the chairs, and do anything that needed to be done. He would often be one of the two or three people who stayed to finish cleaning up after the service as well. Through his years of fame as a baseball player, Alvin remained a model of humility.

In the years since, I've watched Alvin continue to inspire others. He doesn't do it through public speeches much, or by leveraging his baseball persona, but rather through a humble spirit and a servant's heart. I have never once observed him taking advantage of his athletic celebrity status. To me, he is a modern-day Nehemiah.

What about you? What is your leadership style? Do you stay in the ivory tower and direct the troops, or are you a get-down-and-get-dirty type?

In the chapter titled "Focus, People, Focus," I related that I had asked my friends who are ministry leaders to finish this sentence: "I wish my workers would . . ." How would you finish it?

Now let me meddle: Do *you* do what you want your workers to do? Whatever your answer was . . . have *you* modeled it?

Your Example—Your Legacy

I have a final question, and I encourage you to think of an answer before you continue reading. Here's the question: Who do you know that has left a spiritual legacy?

Have you thought of someone? Got a name in mind, or a face? Good. Now hang on to it for a bit.

I urge you never to minimize the potential for what your life's example can do. We've talked about many different ways to motivate people to stay involved in ministry, but if you don't lead by example, the others become ineffective. It's almost like a multiplication problem—I describe it as M x E = S. This stands for Methods (of leadership) x Example = Success.

If you excel at all six other methods for motivating that I've listed in this book, but your example is a zero, your leadership equation looks like this: 6 x 0 = 0. Do you get what I'm saying?

Let's say you get three of the others down, but you really shine as an example (say you are a 5), then your equation looks like this: 3 x 5 = 15. Don't ever underestimate the importance of your example.

> There are many other ways to motivate people to stay involved in ministry, but if you don't lead by example, the others become ineffective.

Now . . . whom did you name that left a spiritual legacy? A nationally known spiritual leader, like Billy Graham or Rick Warren? How about a pastor of a church? How about someone in your family—like maybe your grandmother? How about a children's worker or youth worker who showed a special interest in you or others?

I've asked that question often. In my own private, non-scientific way of surveying, I can say that hands down, the majority of respondents name a family member. In fact, if the person I'm asking begins to choke up, I know they are about to name a dad or mom or grandpa or grandma. The second most frequently mentioned category is the children's worker or youth worker who genuinely cared about the kids he or she served. Rarely—maybe 1 out of 20 times—will someone mention a prominent spiritual leader.

Lindsey Woods, a ministry friend from Missouri, answered my question this way:

> My father pastored a small church in the St. Louis area when I was in middle school. His church secretary was a one-woman show when it came to our children's ministry,

Example · 173

and to this day, I credit her, alongside my parents, for giving me a love for the Word. I remember that on Wednesday nights, there were only four children: my sister, me, and two from one other family. But she spent an enormous amount of time preparing. She helped us create our very own Bible dictionaries, and then we created our own little maps of Paul's journeys. She gave me a love for studying God's Word, and I have never forgotten that.

It's also true for me. Ask me that question, and my immediate answer is "my mom." No one has been a greater example to me than she has. Only a few people outside our family know Margaret Fowler. She lives in a small, rural town, attends a very small church, and now that she is in her 90s, many of her friends have already passed away. But her family knows her. Her 3 children (that includes me, of course), 6 grandchildren, and 19 (and counting) great-grandchildren all have been deeply affected by her example.

Mom is exemplary in her devotional life. At 92, she faithfully studies Scripture and continues to learn. She reviews regularly the hundreds of Scripture verses that she has committed to memory over her life. She is faithful in her prayers for all of us and deeply concerned about the souls of all of her family and neighbors.

Mom is exemplary in her service. Though she now lives on Social Security, she gives significantly to missions and has for decades. Up until just a couple of months ago, she still taught a women's Bible study in her town. She plays the piano in her little country church.

Mom is also exemplary in her worldview. She sees her own actions and those of others through the lens of Scriptural truth, and she encourages all of us to do the same.

We, her family, are all fiercely loyal to her. That extends beyond children to the in-laws, grandchildren and great-grandchildren. Of one thing I am certain: Her family won't quit on her before God calls her home.

The principle applies to ministry, too. When you are that kind of example to others in ministry, they will respond by being loyal to you. While our transient society pretty much guarantees that some people will move away, your batting average for keeping workers will be incredibly high if you live a life of exemplary godliness before your people.

Nehemiah's example was one of exemplary godliness as well. His strong confidence in God, his transparent burden, his careful planning, his unmovable determination in the face of opposition— all of these attributes motivated the workers to miraculously complete a monumental task.

God might use you in a similar way if your life is also characterized by exemplary godliness. Maybe your sphere of influence will be your family and small circle of friends—like my mother's has been. Maybe it will extend nationally or worldwide. Leave that to Him. Focus on who you are in God, and then follow Nehemiah's pattern in leading those workers He has given to you.

Here's my final advice—this should sound pretty familiar by now, but the principles bear repeating:

Pray as first response.
Get families to serve together.
Focus on the right issues.
Help people find meaning in ministry.
Equip for work, and equip for war.
Connect people to the vision and to one another.
Walk your talk.

Do these things, and, like Nehemiah, you will no doubt leave a legacy that inspires others to serve God well.

Plus, fewer of your workers will quit.

Think and Talk About It

1. Can you think of an example from your experience of something that was a cultural humiliation and therefore hurt God's reputation?

Example   175

2. What drives you to be culturally excellent in ministry? Why do you say that?

3. Can you share a story about someone who goes beyond what is expected to serve others? How does that make you feel about serving with them?

4. How do you serve those who are under you organizationally?

5. Without giving names or betraying confidences, can you think of examples of ministry leaders who were or who were not sacrificial in their leadership? How did their styles make those under them feel?

6. How do you set an example for those who serve with you?

7. What do you want your ministry legacy to be?

Notes

1. *International Standard Bible Encyclopedia,* vol. 1 (Grand Rapids, MI: Wm. B. Eerdmans Publishing, 1979), p. 837.

2. *The Good News: A Magazine of Understanding.* http://www.gnmagazine.org/issues/gn21/archaeologyexile.htm.

3. Gene Getz, *Nehemiah: Becoming a Disciplined Leader* (Nashville, TN: Broadman and Holman Publishers, 1995), p. 23.

4. Raymond Brown, *The Message of Nehemiah* (Downers Grove, IL: InterVarsity Press, 1998), p. 56.

ALSO BY
LARRY FOWLER

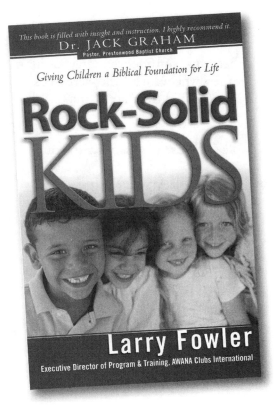

This book is filled with insight and instruction. I highly recommend it.
Dr. JACK GRAHAM
Pastor, Prestonwood Baptist Church

Giving Children a Biblical Foundation for Life

Rock-Solid
KIDS

Larry Fowler
Executive Director of Program & Training, AWANA Clubs International

Rock-Solid Kids
ISBN 978.08307.37130
ISBN 08307.37138

Sometimes children are viewed in terms of their future value. But to Jesus, children were precious in the here and now, and He gave them His full attention and love. We must view children in the same way. Whether your children's ministry is in your home or in your church, *Rock-Solid Kids* will help you build a strong ministry modeled on scriptural teaching. This unique examination of the biblical basis for children's ministry includes eight core chapters. Each chapter is based on one or more Scripture passages and covers topics such as the importance, responsibility, content and golden opportunity of children's ministry. The "foundation rocks" in this book are exactly what teachers and parents need to help them develop a set of convictions—based solidly on the Word of God—for teaching children about the Christian faith.